FAIR RECRUITMENT AND SELECTION

Gerard Lemos has held various senior management posts in major housing associations and is founder and director of Lemos Associates, advising and training on management and equal opportunities both in public and private sector organizations.

FAIR RECRUITMENT AND SELECTION

Gerard Lemos

GUIDES TO MANAGING DIVERSITY

LEMOS ASSOCIATES
LONDON

Published in Great Britain 1994 by

Lemos Associates
20 Pond Square
London N6 6BA

Telephone 081-348 8263

© Lemos Associates 1994

No part of this publication may be
reproduced or transmitted in any form or
by any means, electronically or
mechanically, including photocopying,
recording and information storage or
retrieval system, without prior permission
in writing from the publisher.

ISBN 1-898001-02-2

A CIP catalogue record for this book is
available from the British Library

Cover design by Mick Keates
Phototypeset by Kerrypress Ltd, Luton
Printed by BPC Wheatons Ltd, Exeter

CONTENTS

1	INTRODUCTION	1
	Users of the guide	2
	Contents summary	3
	Part I Organizational framework	5
1	EQUAL OPPORTUNITIES POLICIES	7
	Legal imperatives	7
	Pragmatic reasons	8
	Ethical considerations	9
	Positive action and positive discrimination	11
	Beyond fair recruitment and selection	12
2	LAW AND PRACTICE FOR FAIR RECRUITMENT AND SELECTION	14
	General	15
	Race Relations Act 1976	15
	Sex Discrimination Act 1975	17
	Shared provisions in the Sex Discrimination Act and the Race Relations Act	18
	Fair Employment (Northern Ireland) Act 1989	19
	Disabled Persons (Employment) Act 1944	20
	Unlawful discrimination in recruitment	22
	Genuine occupational qualifications	24
	Advertising	25
	Interviews	27
	Selection	27
	Positive action	29
	Case studies	30

3	TRAINING FOR RECRUITERS	36
	Equal opportunities	36
	Fair recruitment and selection	37
	Specimen programme	38
	Competencies required	40
	Part II Recruitment and selection process	43
4	JOB ANALYSIS	45
	Areas to be analysed	46
	Stereotyping in recruitment	50
5	JOB DESCRIPTIONS AND PERSON SPECIFICATIONS	53
	Drafting a job description	53
	Drafting a person specification	54
6	ATTRACTING A FIELD OF CANDIDATES	57
	Internal versus external advertising	58
	Institutions, schemes, agencies and media	59
	Information to inquirers	64
	Application forms	65
	Curricula vitae	66
7	JOB ADVERTISEMENTS	67
	Advertisements which deter applications	68
	Equal opportunities statements	69
	Targeted advertising	69
	Advertising for members of a particular race or sex	73
	Advertising for people with disabilities	74
	Advertising through community networks	74
8	SHORTLISTING	75
	Who should shortlist?	75
	Length of shortlist	76
	Shortlisting techniques	76
	Planning and running an assessment centre	80
	Choosing the right tests	81
	Avoiding discriminatory tests	82
	Weighting the tests	84
	Evaluating an assessment centre	86

9	INTERVIEWING	88
	Interview panel members	88
	Preparing for interviews	89
	Interview questioning	93
	Listening skills	98
	Endings	99
	Unstated prejudices	99
10	OTHER METHODS OF ASSESSING CANDIDATES	102
	Psychometric tests	102
	References	106
11	SELECTING THE SUCCESSFUL CANDIDATE	112
12	MONITORING AND TARGET-SETTING	115
	Record-keeping and monitoring	115
	Targets	117
	Part III Appendices	119
A	HUMAN RESOURCES DOCUMENTATION	120
	1 Person specifications	121
	2 Application form	124
	3 CV cover sheet	128
	4 Applicant's shortlisting list	129
	5 Interview record form	130
	6 Monitoring form	131
B	CODES OF PRACTICE	133
	1 Extracts on recruitment and selection from the CRE code of practice	133
	2 Extracts on recruitment and selection from the EOC code of practice	138
C	GLOSSARY	144
	INDEX	147

ACKNOWLEDGEMENTS

Permission from the Equal Opportunities Commission and the Commission for Racial Equality is gratefully acknowledged to reproduce the extracts from their codes of practice on employment which appear in appendix B of this guide.

INTRODUCTION

A successful organization will be one which has a workforce that is built on a wide range of skills, experiences, abilities and backgrounds. The workforce will also be sufficiently diverse to meet the needs of the widest cross-section of customers, potential customers and members of the public. Recruitment and selection practices which result in a workforce that does not have this diversity are hampering the capacity of an organization to realise its full potential.

Recruitment and selection decisions are possibly, therefore, the most important decisions that managers must take. Mistakes in recruitment and selection often prove costly. Poor performance by an inappropriate recruit may result in under-achievement, disciplinary problems, the cost of staff cover, further recruitment costs, industrial tribunal cases and so on.

Perversely, this is also an area in which managers are often given remarkably little guidance and training. It is also all too often a task that is approached casually, without adequate preparation, or procedures. Decisions are made on subjective hunches, without supporting evidence and disastrous consequences are almost inevitable.

Fair recruitment and selection is about getting the right person for the job. It is also about not unnecessarily or unwittingly excluding suitably qualified people from applying or being considered for the job. This is not only to their benefit, but is also a way of ensuring that the organization is recruiting from the largest pool of available talent. So being fair is also the best way to get the right person for the job.

Users of the guide

This guide is for all managers who are involved in recruitment and selection, not just personnel or human resources specialists. It provides a structured, systematic and objective approach to recruitment. If followed, the guidance in this book will help managers not only to make the right decisions, but also support the decision they have made by displaying a process that is transparent and demonstrably fair.

Contents summary

Part I sets out the organizational framework for fair recruitment and selection. Chapters 1 and 2 inform recruiters about equal opportunities policies and the relevant legislation which aim to ensure that discrimination does not take place in employment. Chapter 3 deals with the training needs of managers and others in the organization who have a role to play in fair recruitment and selection. It provides suggestions of programmes and objectives.

Part II deals with the process of recruitment and selection. This starts with chapter 4 which sets out the approach and the format for effective job analysis when posts become vacant or when new posts are created. Chapter 5 considers the best method of drawing up person and job specifications so as to ensure that clear, measurable selection criteria are set against which candidates can be judged. Chapters 6 and 7 identify best practice in advertising jobs and the implications for fair selection of other methods of attracting a field of candidates. Chapter 8 goes on to consider the application form and the process of shortlisting.

Chapter 9 defines different types of interview questions and ways of ensuring that the appropriate information is sought during interviews to enable recruiters to make objective selection decisions. Chapter 10 identifies other non-discriminatory selection techniques through which recruiters may judge the skills or knowledge of a candidate. Chapter 11 sets out criteria for approaches to choosing successful candidates which are objective and consistent. Chapter 12 considers the need to monitor and set targets for equality in recruitment and selection.

Specimen human resources documentation for use in day-to-day practice is set out in Part III, together with the sections on recruitment and selection from the codes of practices produced by the Commission for Racial Equality and the Equal Opportunities Commission.

PART I

ORGANIZATIONAL FRAMEWORK

CHAPTER 1

EQUAL OPPORTUNITIES POLICIES

Fair recruitment and selection needs to be seen as part of an organization's wider commitment to equality of opportunity in employment and managing diversity within the workforce. A commitment to equal opportunities is essential to the health and success of the organization from three separate perspectives - legally, pragmatically and ethically.

Legal imperatives

The details of the relevant legislation are covered in chapter 2. The relevant sections of the statutory codes of practice on employment issued by the Commission for Racial Equality (CRE) and the Equal Opportunities Commission (EOC) are also included in Part III. A good employer will see compliance with the law as the foundation stone for good practice.

It is only on the grounds of race and sex - colour, nationality or ethnic origin, gender and marital status - that individuals are protected by law from discrimination in employment. Employers, may through their equal opportunities policies debar discrimination by their employees on other grounds, for example, discrimination on the grounds of age, sexual orientation or disability. Discrimination on these grounds would, however, not break the law other than in exceptional circumstances.

Pragmatic reasons

From a pragmatic point of view an organization bent upon success will want to ensure that it recruits the best people available. If members of some groups are unfairly discriminated against, or excluded, or believe that they may be discriminated against and therefore do not apply, the organization has unnecessarily restricted the pool of talent from which it is seeking staff. A `rigged market' has been created detrimental not only to the interests of the individuals thereby denied employment opportunities, but also to the free entry of talented people into the organization.

A successful organization will also seek to ensure that staff have achieved the highest level of motivation, without which they will not fulfil their potential either in terms of learning or performance, and so add the maximum value to their organization through their efforts and in return for their remuneration. Staff who feel that they are being discriminated against or unfairly treated are unlikely to be able to function to their full potential. Their morale will be affected, and then their performance.

Poor performance may lead to formal disciplinary action, which will exacerbate the low morale, and a vicious, downward spiral of poor morale and performance will have been created which is likely to culminate in extreme cases in that person leaving the organization, sometimes unwillingly. This will not only influence their views of the organization's commitments to equality of opportunity, but also all those other people, perhaps outside the organization, with whom they discuss their experiences, who may then feel discouraged from applying for jobs in that organization themselves.

Not only will the morale of those individuals be affected, but also a tacit acceptance by managers to tolerate unfair treatment or harassment will lead other members of staff to conclude that maverick management does not know what it wants, is happy to see people being unfairly treated and may at some stage in the future treat them unfairly as well. This may in turn affect their morale and motivation.

Ethical considerations

The third set of reasons why equal opportunities policies are important in organizational life are ethical ones. Unfair treatment of any group is likely to affect and possibly offend not only those whose opportunities are curtailed, but also some of those who are supposedly in the privileged group, or the group which enjoys the advantage, even though they may not realise it. Those who are being discriminated against or unfairly treated may well be angry and resentful, making others feel guilty, suspicious or confused.

For the others - white people, men, those without disabilities, for example - who feel ill at ease or offended by unfair treatment they witness, this may result in either their complaining or seeking to change the practices which lead to unfair treatment. This would be a positive outcome. Real change and movement towards greater equality can only come about in organizations as a result of an alliance between the individuals or groups who are disadvantaged and those individuals or groups who are powerful or influential within the organization.

A less positive outcome would be if members of staff who are offended by unfair treatment say nothing and their silence is taken as evidence of indifference or acceptance. They are likely to become disaffected with the leadership of the organization, or cynical about any commitments the organization has publicly made to equality of opportunity. It will be seen by one and all as mere lip service. The leadership of the organization will then find it hard to argue that while the stated rules on equality of opportunity can be broken with impunity, procedures in other areas must be followed to the letter.

The values of the organization, including non-discrimination and equality of opportunity can only be made a reality and implemented by staff if there is a general knowledge and understanding of what is expected which concurs with their own personal integrity. If organizations recruit staff who are unconcerned about the organization's ethics or indeed actively hostile to them, they are unlikely to be effective members of the team. For teams to be successful, they do not all have to be the same; they do however have to some shared understandings and perspectives on the world and the place of the organization in it. In short, all members of staff need to feel a responsibility for treating applicants for jobs, enquirers about the organization's services, colleagues and customers - both internal and external regardless of race or other differences - at least as well as they would expect to be treated themselves.

Positive action and positive discrimination

One objective of fair recruitment and selection is to remove unfair, albeit often unintentional, bias in recruitment. A broader objective is to achieve a workforce that represents the wider community in which they work. This may be achieved simply by removing unfair or unnecessary impediments as discussed later. However, there will be circumstances where black or ethnic minority people, women or people with disabilities will need more assistance than simply the removal of unfair barriers. This is not because they are inferior, more stupid or less able, but because experiences in the education system, or elsewhere at work have prevented them from getting the knowledge, skills or qualifications to qualify as serious contenders for the particular job. They may therefore need specific encouragement in advertisements or through other means to apply for jobs, or they may require training to allow them to acquire the knowledge, skills or experience to allow them to compete on an equal footing.

To discriminate positively, or give preferential treatment to less well-qualified or skilled candidates because they are members of groups which have been previously under-represented or excluded, is unlikely to be a good idea. It may to lead to considerable bad feeling amongst those who are `advantaged' but had not, until that moment, realised it. The person who benefits will undoubtedly enjoy a short-term material advantage. However preferential treatment is unlikely to be in their interest in the medium or longer term. It may turn out that they are not up to the job, in which case they may well lose it, and along with the job lose a great deal of self-confidence. They may also find that their colleagues harbour resentments which make it harder for them to do their new job effectively, or to become a member of the team. They may also make it considerably more difficult for other members of their community to enter that workplace group without being tarnished with the reputation by association of preferential treatment and limited competence.

There will always be those who say that a woman, or a black person only got the job because they were a woman or were black. These views have to be isolated by managers and colleagues, and the successful individual needs the confidence to know that they were appointed to their job fairly and squarely on the basis of their competence. In short, no one regardless of race, gender or any other consideration should be given a job they cannot do.

Beyond fair recruitment and selection

Too many managers in too many organizations regard equal opportunities in employment as being only about recruitment and selection. There are, of course, many other aspects of equal opportunities. An effective equal opportunities strategy will incorporate alongside fairness in recruitment and selection effective induction into both the formal and the informal working practices of the organization, fairness in career development and promotion, access to training opportunities, creating a work environment free of harassment and in which the dignity of all is respected.

The link between fair recruitment and selection and career development is important to stress. Organizations which wish to change the make-up of their workforce will clearly need to offer their jobs for external competition in order to draw in people from different backgrounds from outside the organization.

This may leave the existing workforce feeling aggrieved, particularly if in the past internal promotion was the order of the day. Alongside fair recruitment and selection, therefore, organizations need to be committed to providing existing staff with training and career development opportunities that prepare them to compete for promotion or development opportunities, not for automatic promotion on a `Buggin's turn' basis.

CHAPTER 2

LAW AND PRACTICE FOR FAIR RECRUITMENT AND SELECTION

It may not always be possible to have a human resources or personnel specialist present at all stages of the recruitment process. Many other people will be involved - receptionists, managers and others working on shortlisting, interviewing and selecting - they might all unwittingly, or deliberately break the laws on discrimination. It is imperative therefore that knowledge in this area is spread beyond the experts. Organizations will obviously want to avoid unnecessary industrial tribunal cases and other legal challenges. The best organizations will also want to ensure that they are complying with best practice, and the law must be the starting point for setting standards of best practice in any area.

This chapter is structured as a series of questions and answers. It is designed to deal with particular concerns, misconceptions or lack of knowledge that managers may have about the legislation, rather than leaving them to extract specific answers from discursive prose.

The main statutes covered in this chapter are the Race Relations Act 1976, the Sex Discrimination Act 1975, the

Fair Employment (Northern Ireland) Act 1989, and the Disabled Persons (Employment) Act 1944.

The last section sets out some case studies which show how the law has been interpreted in practice. These too are set out as questions for the reader to consider, with the findings of the court or tribunal following on.

General

■ *Against which groups is it unlawful to discriminate in this country?*

Discrimination is only unlawful on the grounds of race, sex or marital status.

■ *Do the same laws apply all over the United Kingdom?*

No. The Race Relations Act does not apply in Northern Ireland. There is separate specific legislation - the Fair Employment (Northern Ireland) Act 1989. The Sex Discrimination Act applies all over the United Kingdom, although there are specific exclusions on the grounds of national security and the protection of public order in Northern Ireland.

Race Relations Act 1976

■ *What is covered by the term racial discrimination?*

Discrimination on the grounds of:

Colour	Yes
Race	Yes
Religion	Not in mainland Britain, except where membership of a religious group denotes sharing a common national or ethnic origin such as

16   Fair Recruitment and Selection

	sikhs. For the purposes of the Race Relations Act catholics or protestants would not constitute racial groups. In certain circumstances discrimination against jewish people is unlawful. Religious discrimination is unlawful in Northern Ireland.
Nationality	Yes
Place of birth	No, unless it discloses race or ethnic origin
Race of parents	No
Ethnic origin	Yes
National origin	Yes
Cultural habits	No.

■ *Does the Race Relations Act 1976 only protect black people and members of ethnic minorities from discrimination?*

No. The Act covers all races. There have been several prosecutions against organizations for discriminating against white people.

■ *Are any special duties placed on any specific organizations?*

Yes. Local authorities have a specific duty to eliminate unlawful racial discrimination, promote equality of opportunity and good race relations under section 71 of the Race Relations Act 1976. The same duty is placed on the Housing Corporation by section 56 of the Housing Act 1988.

■ *Who is responsible for enforcing the Race Relations Act?*

The Commission for Racial Equality has statutory powers to investigate and to serve statutory non-discrimination notices. Employment matters are dealt with in industrial tribunals and other matters in the courts.

Sex Discrimination Act 1975

■ *What is covered by the term sex discrimination?*

Discrimination against:

Women	Yes
Men	Yes
Married people	Yes, but only in employment
Single people	No
Gay men	No
Lesbians	No

■ *Is it legal to pay men and women different wages for doing the same job?*

No. This would be direct sex discrimination.

■ *Is it legal to pay different wages for jobs which are not the same but have equivalent value to the organization?*

No. Equal pay legislation provides that employers have to give equal pay for work of equal value, even where the jobs are not the same, only broadly similar.

■ *Are there any other circumstances where discrimination is permissible?*

It is possible to have men or women only private clubs. Women are also not permitted to work full-time down the mines and in other specific circumstances.

Discrimination in recruitment of people to work in an employer's home is also permissible.

■ *Who is responsible for enforcing the Sex Discrimination Act?*

The Equal Opportunities Commission has statutory powers to investigate when they receive complaints. Employment matters are dealt with in industrial tribunals while other kinds of discrimination are dealt with by the courts.

Shared provisions in the Sex Discrimination Act 1975 and Race Relations Act 1976

■ *Does the Race Relations Act and the Sex Discrimination Act protect only individuals or does it also apply to groups?*

Both statutes cover individuals as well as groups. Decisions apply to workplaces of all members of any group within the area of jurisdiction of the court or tribunal.

■ *Is discrimination unlawful only when it is intentional?*

No. The law considers discriminatory effects or results, regardless of the intentions. Ignorance of the law is also no defence with this legislation as with any other.

■ *Who is responsible in a court or tribunal if an employer has instructed an employee to discriminate?*

Both the employer and the employee are potentially liable. Generally it is the employer against whom action is taken.

■ *Who is responsible where an employee discriminates without the knowledge of their employer?*

Again, both the employer and employee are potentially liable. This is known as the liability of principals and is a general rule of law. It also occurs in health and safety at work legislation. In order avoid liability the employer would have to demonstrate that all reasonable steps had been taken to ensure that their employees did not discriminate. This is likely to include training staff, and monitoring the implementation of equal opportunities policies.

■ *Is racial or sexual harassment, at work or elsewhere, unlawful?*

Although not explicitly identified under the Race Relations Act or the Sex Discrimination Act, case-law has now laid down that both sexual and racial harassment can constitute unlawful direct discrimination where an individual is treated less favourably and where they suffer a detriment as a result of the treatment.

Fair Employment (Northern Ireland) Act 1989

■ *What is covered by this statute?*

The legislation deals with discrimination on the grounds of religion only in this part of the UK. Its aims are to encourage:
1) active practice of fair employment by employers;

2)   close and continuous audit of that practice by new and stronger enforcement agencies;
3)   use of affirmative actions, goals and timetables to remedy under-representation of individual religious groups;
4)   use of criminal penalties and economic sanctions to ensure good employment practices.

■ *What duties are placed on employers in Northern Ireland?*

1)   compulsory registration of all public employers and private employers with a workforce of more than 10 employees;
2)   compulsory monitoring of the religion of the staff of all registered employers and the monitoring of applications for employment to all public employers and private employers of 250 or more;
3)   compulsory reviews of recruitment, training and promotion practices to determine if fair participation in the concern is provided for the members of the religious communities with auditing by the Fair Employment Commission, the statutory body responsible for implementation of the legislation;
4)   mandatory affirmative action, and goals and timetables as directed by the Fair Employment Commission.

The Disabled Persons (Employment) Act 1944

■ *Is it illegal to discriminate against people with disabilities?*

No. There is no specific protection for people with disabilities as there is for those discriminated against on the grounds of race or sex (or religion in Northern Ireland).

■ *Do employers have any other particular responsibilities towards people with disabilities?*

Yes. Employers with 20 or more staff have a duty to employ a quota of registered disabled people, which is three per cent of their total workforce. Without an exemption certificate, an employer will have to give all vacancies that arise to people with disabilities until the quota is met.

■ *What if a suitably qualified registered disabled person cannot be found who meets the job description?*

There are a number of recruitment strategies that can be explored in order to find a suitably qualified registered disabled person, such as contacting local job centres. But if a suitable person cannot be found, it is possible to get a permit from the local job centre exempting an organization from the quota system. These can be obtained either to fill current vacancies or, as a bulk permit, to allow staff to be hired for a period of up to six months. Even if the organization holds a bulk permit, however, the local job centre must still be notified of any vacancies in case a suitable registered disabled person becomes available.

■ *What is the designated employment scheme?*

It is a scheme whereby certain occupations, such as car park attendant, are reserved for registered disabled persons.

■ *Do large companies have any special responsibilities toward people with disabilities?*

Yes. The Companies Act 1985 makes companies with, on average, over 250 employees include in their annual reports information about their policies on people with disabilities in the past financial year. Companies must ensure that they give fair consideration to people with disabilities who apply for jobs, that they continue to employ anyone who becomes disabled while working for the company, and that training and career development is provided for employees with disabilities.

Unlawful discrimination in recruitment

■ *Is discrimination permissible in recruitment?*

No. The Sex Discrimination Act and the Race Relations Act both make it unlawful for employers to discriminate on the grounds of sex or race in the selection of employees. Discrimination in recruitment is unlawful, since it is the first step in the selection process. Non-discriminatory recruitment practices aim to ensure that no applicant group is discouraged from applying.

■ *What is the difference between direct and indirect discrimination in recruitment?*

Direct discrimination occurs when someone is treated less favourably because of their race or sex. Indirect discrimination occurs when an unnecessary condition that may at first seem fair because it applies to all, in practice puts members of one group at a greater disadvantage. For instance, demanding fluent spoken

English for a job on a production line is indirect discrimination since the ability to speak English is not necessary to do the job. Both forms of discrimination are unlawful.

Indirect discrimination in recruitment can occur as a result of seeking applicants from a limited pool that includes only, or mainly, members of one race or sex. For example, advertising for a swimming coach by putting up notices in only the men's changing rooms of local pools is indirect discrimination. Specifying that the coach must be male would be direct discrimination. The CRE code of practice also states that employers must be able to justify their recruitment methods. If a recruitment policy reduces the number of applicants from a particular racial group, it is indirectly discriminatory. (See appendix B below.)

There are, however, two exceptions in which selection on the grounds of race or sex is allowed: if the work is outside Great Britain and a person of a particular nationality is required; or if there is a genuine occupational qualification (see below) for the person recruited to be of a particular sex, race, colour, ethnic or national origin.

■ *Does the law allow an employer to discriminate positively in favour of black and ethnic minority people at the expense of white people, or women at the expense of men in selecting staff?*

Generally positive discrimination is illegal. However, there are some special cases where it is allowed, for example, where membership of a particular racial group or sex constitutes a genuine occupational qualification, and where that member of staff will be providing a personal service which promotes the welfare of members of that race or sex.

Positive discrimination simply with a view to increasing the numbers of people from a particular racial group or sex in the workforce or among service users is unlawful.

Genuine occupational qualifications

■ *What is a genuine occupational qualification?*

Under section 5 of the Race Relations Act, people of a particular race may be chosen for reasons of authenticity for dramatic performances, photographic or artistic modelling, or employment in an 'ethnic restaurant'. In addition, a particular racial, ethnic or national origin may be stipulated if the job involves providing personal or face-to-face services to members of a racial group. These services must be for the welfare or good of the members of the group and they must be services that can best be provided by another member of that group.

There is a genuine occupational qualification for a job only if it can be objectively proven by the employer. The CRE recommends that the racial group should be defined as precisely as possible to show that there is a cultural, linguistic or ethnic link between the two groups. So in advertising for a social worker to liaise with West African children in children's homes, being black would not make someone genuinely qualified for the job since a person of West African origin could best provide the services.

Under the Sex Discrimination Act, genuine occupational qualifications include dramatic performances and artistic and photographic modelling. Being male is a genuine occupational qualification for certain jobs outside the UK in countries whose laws and customs would make it unacceptable for the job to be performed by a woman. The other main genuine occupational qualification concerns preserving privacy and decency. So in an all-male institution, being a man may be a genuine occupational qualification if decency is to be preserved.

■ *What impact does a genuine occupational qualification have on recruitment and selection?*

Where a job has a genuine occupational qualification that the postholder must be of a particular sex or race, it is not discriminatory for the employer to choose an employee on the basis of sex or race. For example, authenticity can be a genuine occupational qualification for an Indian restaurant who may advertise for waiters and waitresses of Indian origin. The chef, who is not seen by the customers, does not come under the rule of authenticity and so may be of any race, so long, of course, as he or she can cook the required Indian dishes.

Advertising

■ *Does the term advertising just cover what appears in newspapers?*

No. Advertising is defined broadly to include everything from notices in shop windows to newspaper advertisements, whether or not it is directed at the general public.

■ *Can advertising for jobs be discriminatory?*

Yes. If it is, both the employer and the publisher are responsible. To test if an advertisement is discriminatory, the question is whether the text or illustration can be understood by a reasonable person to show an intention to discriminate. If so, simply adding an equal opportunities statement will not change the discriminatory nature of the advertisement.

Under the Sex Discrimination Act, job descriptions with a 'sexual connotation', such as waitress or postman, are considered to show an intention to discriminate unless the advertisement states that persons of either sex will be considered for the post. While within the law, such job titles are best avoided, since they may discourage applicants from one sex or the other. Men might be discouraged from applying for the post of 'tea lady (m/f)', while women might not apply to become 'salesman (m/f)'. Gender-neutral terms like tea server or salesperson are therefore more appropriate.

■ *What types of advertisements may be construed as discriminatory?*

The test is whether the advertisement might reasonably be thought to be discriminatory by an ordinary person. It is therefore essential to compose advertisements carefully, being sure that neither the words nor the pictures used could imply an intention to discriminate. A statement that applicants of both sexes and of all races, national and ethnic origins are welcome should also be included. Only the EOC or the CRE can bring proceedings if an advertisement is discriminatory. But individuals can institute proceedings alleging discrimination in recruitment proceedings based on the content of the advertisement.

■ *Is advertising targeted at a particular racial group or gender permitted if that group is under-represented?*

Yes. Advertisements directed at members of one sex or race are permitted, so long as they clearly indicate that there is no intention to discriminate against members of other groups. The advertisements may also be placed in sections of the press mainly read by the under-represented group.

Interviews

■ *Can interview questions discriminate or put candidates at an unfair disadvantage?*

Yes. If the question is not relevant, or if it sets an unrealistically high standard, or if a member of another racial group or sex would not have been asked the question.

■ *What kinds of interview questions should be asked in order to avoid discrimination?*

Interview questions should relate directly to the job. They should be non-discriminatory and should not give the impression of discrimination. For example, female applicants with children should not be singled out for questioning about their childcare arrangements, unless the same question is also asked of male applicants.

Selection

■ *Is it lawful to discriminate at the point of selection?*

No. While the law allows under-represented groups (see below) to be encouraged to apply for jobs, it does not allow sex or race to be a factor in the decision to select someone for employment. That would be unlawful discrimination.

28　Fair Recruitment and Selection

■ *Must arrangements for selection be non-discriminatory?*

Yes. Employers must not discriminate on the grounds of sex or race in the arrangements that they make for selecting staff. Even if the arrangements, such as application forms, tests or interviews, were not made with the intention of being discriminatory, if, in practice, they prove to cause discrimination, they are unlawful.

■ *What kind of selection criteria should be used to prevent discrimination?*

The selection criteria should be clear, objective and relevant, specific to the job, and aimed at the right level. They should avoid unjustifiable tests, such as language or other tests which might be discriminatory because they filter out otherwise qualified minority applicants.

■ *To correct an imbalance, can sex or race be used as the criteria for selection?*

No. To select on the basis of sex or race is unlawful discrimination. Imbalances and under-representation (see below) should be corrected using pre-application training and advertisements to encourage minority members to apply. Under-represented groups may be given special training to enable them to apply for particular work. The training cannot, however, be a condition of employment - that would be discrimination if only the members of one sex or race were allowed to take part in the training programme. Selecting employees must be done separately. Apprenticeships do not count as training schemes but as employment, and so cannot be offered on the basis of race or sex, even where under-representation exists.

■ *Can women be excluded from recruitment or promotion because they are pregnant?*

No. This would be direct sex discrimination.

Positive action

■ *What is under-representation?*

Under-representation is a legal term which is defined differently in the Race Relations Act and the Sex Discrimination Act. According to the Race Relations Act, a group is under-represented if the people doing the work at a particular establishment are either exclusively from one racial group or make up a smaller proportion of either the entire workforce or of the people in the general population from which the workforce is recruited. The definition in the Sex Discrimination Act is broader, since it is not restricted to people working for one company or organization, but to people doing a particular job in the whole of the UK. Members of one sex are under-represented if, within the past twelve months, no member of that sex has done the work or if the proportion is comparatively small.

■ *If black or ethnic minority people or women are under-represented in the workforce, are employers allowed to give them any special assistance?*

Yes. Employers cannot positively discriminate in favour of those groups when appointing people to jobs. However, employers may take positive action measures to allow people from those groups to compete more equally and to redress past disadvantages. For example, employers can provide special training schemes for women or black and ethnic minority people if those groups are under-represented, but employers cannot discriminate at the point of selection for a non-trainee vacancy.

Recruitment advertising can also be targeted in ways likely to encourage members of under-represented groups to apply - either by the contents of the advertisement, or where it is placed.

■ *How can the number of applicants for jobs from minority or under-represented groups be increased within the law?*

The best way to increase the number of minority applicants is to recruit from job centres, careers offices and schools which serve members of more than one sex, race, colour or ethnic or national origin. Seeking new employees by word of mouth or through a trade union, if most of the employees or union members are from the same racial group, will not broaden the applicant base. In addition, placing advertisements in the ethnic minority or women's press, and the journals for people with disabilities may also help.

Positive action statements on advertisements such as, `we positively welcome applicants from .... because they are under-represented within the workforce/at this grade' also have a significant impact in encouraging members of under-represented groups to apply.

Case studies

The following case studies are given as examples of the law in practice. They seek to illustrate concepts such as indirect discrimination and genuine occupational qualifications. They also seek to illustrate areas of discrimination which may not be against the law, although they may be unfair. The reader should consider in the first instance whether they think that discrimination has taken place, and secondly whether it was against the law.

Case A

A large public sector employer has a rule that no one over the age of 28 can apply for a first line managerial position from an administrative grade, as they would be too old by then to progress all the way up the hierarchy. A woman over the age of 28 applies who has had a career break for child rearing wishes to apply.

Outcome

The case involved the civil service. The tribunal found that an age limit of 28 was indirect sex discrimination. Because, at that time, an average woman had more than two years off for child rearing in their twenties, the age qualification could therefore lead to sex discrimination.

Case B

A company has several applicants for a job as production line supervisor in a factory. It is only advertised internally. All of the people who apply are equally well qualified. All of them are called for interview except one, about whom it is known by some of the workforce that he is both gay and HIV positive. The company says that they are not interviewing this candidate because the workforce has found out about him and already drawn up a petition threatening industrial action should he be appointed.

Outcome

The company involved was a supermarket chain and the job was supervisor on the delicatessen counter. The man was not considered for the post and the case did not reach tribunal. However it would not have been a breach of either the Sex Discrimination Act or the Race Relations Act. There is no law protecting people with AIDS or HIV from discrimination.

It is generally accepted that there is no risk of transmitting AIDS or HIV at work so long as normal health and safety standards are adhered to. There is therefore no reason why any member of current or prospective staff should be asked to disclose whether or not they have HIV or AIDS, or have had a test for it.

Nonetheless some companies now ask applicants to take a test which, if they fail, debars them from selection. This practice is not only illogical because of the minimal risk of infection, but also because it does not take into account the HIV status of the existing workforce. Indeed there are still many people who are not aware that they are HIV positive. There are no foolproof ways of screening out people with HIV or AIDS, nor would there be any justification in so doing.

Some employers may consider it a poor investment to employ someone about whom it is known that they will become ill soon. In fact, not everyone with HIV has gone on to contract AIDS, and even amongst those who have, there is often a time lag of many years before their ability to do their job is affected. In many instances this time lag would be longer than people stay in the job on average in ordinary circumstances.

Case C

A large public sector employer runs a training scheme for a professional qualification for a job with them. Although there are plenty of women on the training scheme, they have not recruited women who have children of pre-school age because they believe that they would not be able to cope with the study and are more likely to need time off when the children get sick and this would interfere with their training.

A woman with children under five who wants to get on the scheme complains that this is sex discrimination.

Outcome

The case involved a health authority and the training scheme was for midwives. The tribunal held that this was unlawful sex discrimination because men were not excluded on the same basis. It made no difference that virtually all the people recruited to the scheme were women with children over the age of five years.

Case D

An under-five's centre in an inner city area advertised for an Afro-Caribbean nursery assistant, citing that it was a genuine occupational qualification for the job to be done by a black person because the job involved caring for the children's hair and skin, liaising with parents and reading the children stories in West Indian dialect. A white Englishman was invited for an interview on the basis of his application, but when the panel found out his racial origin, they told him that because he was not Afro-Caribbean, he would not be considered for the job. He then took action claiming unfair racial discrimination.

Outcome

The industrial tribunal found that reading in dialect and caring for hair and skin were not genuine occupational qualifications because they were not important parts of the job. But on appeal, the Employment Appeal Tribunal concluded that it was not up to tribunals to decide what was or was not an important part of the job. That was up to the employers. The tribunal only had a right to step in where the genuine occupational qualification was clearly a sham, set up to side-step the Race Relations Act. The appeal tribunal therefore found in favour of the centre and concluded that being Afro-Caribbean was a genuine occupational qualification. If being a member of a certain racial or ethnic group is a genuine occupational qualification for any part of the job, then it is a genuine occupational qualification for the post.

Case E

Over half of an inner city borough's tenants were of Asian or Afro-Caribbean origin, and when two vacancies arose in housing management, the council specified that being Asian or Afro-Caribbean was a genuine occupational qualification for doing the jobs. The CRE challenged the council's advertisement, alleging that it was discriminatory because the two posts were managerial and did not involve the provision of personal services.

Outcome

The Court of Appeal found in favour of the CRE. Being of a certain race or ethnic group is only a genuine occupational qualification where there is direct, face-to-face contact between the giver and receiver of the services. Being of a particular race or ethnic origin is therefore not a genuine occupational qualification for managerial jobs which do not involve face-to-face contact with clients.

Case G

A company owning a chain of shops had advertised a job. They had arranged that applicants would first be filtered by a shop manager; those that he chose would be put forward for consideration by the district manager. The shop manager intended that no women should be appointed to the post and therefore did not put any women forward to the district manager for consideration. No women were therefore able to be employed.

Outcome

The result hinged on the arrangements made for recruitment and selection. The company argued that it had not arranged for the shop manager to discriminate and that they were not responsible. But the tribunal found that they were. Since they had arranged for the shop manager to be involved in recruitment and selection, they were responsible for ensuring that he conducted the interviews in a non-discriminatory way.

CHAPTER 3

TRAINING FOR RECRUITERS

It is common for people experienced in, or with expertise of a specific subject to become a manager overnight with little preparation and no training. Management, including recruiting and selecting new staff, is a set of skills which needs to be learnt like any other. They are not inherent, nor is anybody a `natural' manager. However it is common for people to undertake recruitment with no training at all, learning as best they can, as they go. Preparing managers and others for their role as recruiters should be mandatory, as it now is in many organizations.

Equal opportunities

Interviewers are not the only ones who will have an impact on whether or not there is fair recruitment and selection. Equal opportunities training for all staff who come into contact with applicants should ensure that all applicants are made to feel welcome. Gate and reception staff, as well as interviewers, should be told not to treat applicants from one group less favourably than those from another group, and have explained to them the policy of the organization on equal opportunities, and its relevance to them.

A workforce that understands the importance of non-discrimination will not only help an employer to avoid litigation caused by allegations of discrimination, but also will help recruit and retain staff from under-represented groups.

Assumptions about sex and race may result in discrimination during the selection process. So training should focus on ways to avoid making judgements based on racial and sexual stereotypes. Interviewers in particular need to be aware of possible misunderstandings that can occur between people of different cultures. When choosing new employees, they should focus on the selection criteria that have been chosen for the job, not stereotypes or preconceived notions.

Fair recruitment and selection

Anybody with a detailed involvement in recruitment needs have an overview of the whole recruitment process: how it all fits together. They also need to understand the key concepts in the law and ensure that it is not broken unwittingly. Over and above these areas, there are two most important aspects of recruitment in which managers need to develop skills.

The first is the ability to draw up a person specification, requiring both objectivity and the need to be specific in setting measurable standards and criteria. The second requirement is interviewing skills. Most people believe themselves quite erroneously to be good interviewers and good judges of character. As a consequence the wrong questions are asked, the evidence is not elicited of a candidate's skills, and recruiters have to default to their `hunches', `first impressions' and `gut instincts' to make a decision which may critically affect the future success of the organization.

The most effective way to learn interviewing skills by practice through role play. It is even more effective if the role play is recorded on video and played back. Whilst this can be unnerving and discomfiting for the participants, like a lot of other unnerving and discomfiting experiences the learning value is high, sometimes in direct proportion to the discomfort. If one interview is conducted and then replayed on tape, the improvement in the second interview is usually enormous.

Below is a specimen programme and objectives for training on recruitment and selection. It is appropriate for groups of no less than six and no more than 12 members. The programme requires the co-operation of two mock candidates who are not actors but people who would be genuinely eligible to be interviewed if there was a real vacancy. Three observers to give feedback to participants are also needed.

The course works best when there are not only mock interviews, but also job analyses, drawing up person specifications and shortlisting based on actual jobs in the organization with which all participants are reasonably familiar, as well as the use of real but anonymous application forms from previous occasions when jobs were advertised.

Specimen programme

Day 1

9.30   **Introductions**
             Administrative arrangements

	Aims and objectives of course
	Participants' expectations
Session 1	Stereotyping in recruitment
Session 2	Relevant legislation and codes of practice
	(Coffee)
Session 3	Job analysis
	(1.00 Lunch)
Session 4	Job descriptions and person specifications
	(Tea)
Session 5	Job advertisements
	(5.00 End)

Day 2

9.30	Recap on Day 1
Session 1	Shortlisting
	(Coffee)
Session 2	Preparing for the interview
	(1.00 Lunch)
Session 3	Interviewing skills
	(Tea)
Session 4	Selecting a candidate
Session 5	Summary and end

Objectives of the course

1) To inform participants of relevant legislation and the contents of the codes of practice published by the Commission for Racial Equality and the Equal Opportunities Commission which aims to ensure that discrimination does not take place in recruitment.
2) To give participants the necessary skills and the format for effective job analysis when posts become vacant or when new posts are created.
3) To identify the best method of drawing up person and job specifications to eliminate in-built indirect

discrimination or opportunities for direct discrimination.

4) To identify best practice in advertising jobs and to consider the fair selection implications of other methods of attracting a field of candidates.

5) To define different types of interview questions and ways of ensuring that discrimination does not take place during interviews.

6) To practice interviewing skills.

7) To ensure that other assessment methods do not discriminate.

8) To decide on approaches to choosing successful candidates which are objective and consistent and do not discriminate.

Ideally training should be completed before any recruitment is undertaken. At the very least recruitment panels should contain a majority of members who have received detailed training on fair recruitment and selection.

Competencies required

Training should focus on the acquisition of skills. It is helpful also to be clear about the behaviour of recruiters that is the expression of good practice in recruitment and selection. These aspects of behaviour are known as competencies. A suggested list of competencies is given below. They can be used by recruiters to evaluate their own skills and competence in undertaking recruitment, and therefore areas where they still need to develop their practice. They can also be used by trainers, and managers of recruiters as ways of ensuring that all recruiters are behaving in ways that will lead to good recruitment decisions.

The following describes the six competencies required by a manager to recruit for diversity:

1) A clear analysis of the template of skills, experiences and knowledge that is necessary to provide services to all actual and potential customers, both internal and external. Recruitment should be used to fill gaps in the template. Successful candidates should not always reflect the skills, experiences and knowledge (and therefore the shortcomings) of the existing workforce.

2) To be able to clearly and openly display the criteria against which recruitment decisions will be taken.

3) To use assessment techniques effectively to elicit evidence about whether candidates meet all the agreed criteria.

4) Not to make judgements based on stereotypes, or without supporting evidence from the candidate's behaviour.

5) To identify and challenge deviations from expected practice before selection decisions are made.

6) To keep clear, concise and comprehensive records of the basis of selection decisions against agreed criteria.

PART II

RECRUITMENT AND SELECTION PROCESS

CHAPTER 4

JOB ANALYSIS

When a job becomes vacant or a new job is created there is an opportunity to form a clear view of the work that is presently being done and the way it complements work being done elsewhere in the organization. This information is essential before deciding on the right sort of person to fill the job and whether or not the organization could attract them.

Managers often fear leaving posts vacant for too long, and are also conscious of how long the recruitment process can take (rarely less than three months if there is an external advertisement) so there is an understandable urge to press on with filling the job without re-assessing it. However, decisions made in haste will often be repented at leisure when it transpires either that the job did not need filling because there is not enough work to do, or it needed to be filled by a different sort of person to the previous postholder.

Skipping the job analysis part of the process is likely therefore to lead to square pegs in round holes and so frustrate the achievement of the wider objectives of the department or indeed the organization as a whole.

Mistakes cannot always be avoided, but their likelihood can be minimised.

Many organizations, particularly those embarked on programmes of quality assurance and total quality management, have learnt the importance of establishing a culture of looking for continuous improvements in the way the organization works, as well as the type and cost of services that are offered to both internal and external customers.

When an existing member of staff leaves and a new one joins is often the best time to implement changes and improvements. Job analysis is a critical part of the reviewing and improvement process to ensure that anachronistic or irrelevant practices, or ineffective bad habits are not perpetuated for old time's sake.

It will rarely be appropriate for human resources or personnel staff to take the lead on the job analysis. It should ideally be conducted by the person who will directly line manage the successful candidate. The line manager will play the largest part in the recruitment process, and therefore needs the most detailed information. Also, once a candidate has been selected, the line manager will be responsible for the induction of the new member of staff, and for their on-going supervision. Information gained in the job analysis process will be invaluable not only in recruitment, but also in the day-to-day management of the person recruited.

Areas to be analysed

It is often easy to imagine that the manager knows all the information about the job and it is simply a matter of writing it down. However there will be many occasions when the job itself or the way it is being performed has been changed without the manager having a detailed knowledge of the changes. Indeed, when the outgoing postholder has been particularly effective, the manager is most likely to be in the dark about how the job is done. So it is always worth checking with the outgoing postholder; the postholder's supervisor or line manager; other people in the same post; together with internal and external customers of the post.

In conducting a job analysis, the following information needs to be ascertained:
- purpose of the job
- position in the organization
- main duties and responsibilities
- specific tasks
- relationships with others
- organizational factors
- personal factors
- competencies.

The job analysis should however be more detailed than simply a list under the headings above. It should also provide both qualitative and quantitative assessments of the post, its objectives and targets, and its workload.

So, for instance, under the heading of purpose of the job, as far as possible a quantifiable list of general objectives should be established. Sometimes the purpose of a job is given in an extremely vague way such as, 'policy development' or 'supervision'. A fuller account would be more helpful such as, 'policy development to ensure that the organization complies with all relevant health and safety at work legislation'.

Under the heading of position in the organization, it will be sufficient to note the line management arrangements if the postholder does not regularly report to anyone else other than their line manager. However, if on specific matters, a postholder must report to someone else, say the human resources manager, then this should be noted in the job analysis. As organizational structures grow more flexible and less traditionally hierarchical, the need to be clear about all the key accountability lines is ever more critical.

The position is similar for all staff for whom the postholder is responsible, even if it is only for some of the time. A job analysis should list not only those people for whom the postholder is always responsible, but also those for whom either the postholder is responsible in the absence of someone else, or those for whom the postholder is responsible on specific tasks or functions, such as leading a working party. The list should also include freelancers, consultants, suppliers, advisers and contractors who may not be direct employees of the organizations, but for whom the postholder is the key link and the customer on behalf of the organization.

Main duties and responsibilities should include what proportion of the postholders' work is spent on that duty, and where they exist, specific expectations. Training officers could, for instance, be told how many courses they should organize in a year, and on how many of those they should provide the training themselves. The analysis should also indicate limits of authority such as budget ceilings and, where applicable, other people who should be consulted or involved in the performance of a particular duty.

Specific tasks could be more detailed, but it is usually futile to attempt an exhaustive list of all tasks that a postholder has ever or will ever have to perform. The regular specific tasks will suffice, along with how often they have to be performed and how long they take. It is worth at this point checking whether there are manuals or guidance notes which the postholder has been or needs to use. These should be specifically referred to and may need updating.

All other posts or groups or departments with whom the postholder has regular contact, even if it is infrequent, should be noted.

Organizational factors include how the job might relate to other similar jobs elsewhere in the organization or even in the same department. Managers are often surprised to discover that two people who they imagine are doing exactly the same tasks are in fact doing entirely different ones because their jobs have evolved differently to take account of the particular organizational circumstances in which they are working.

Impending restructuring, regrading, relocation or other organizational changes might also be included in organizational factors. Recruitment and selection is a key function in managing change and planning for the future of the organization, so to ignore known, likely or possible changes would be foolhardy.

Personal factors should note the levels of knowledge, skill and experience that is necessary to do the job and where the knowledge and skills can be acquired. These factors should be objective and not rely solely on postholder's own assessment. People often tend to imagine that their jobs require a higher level of skills than in fact they do, and often a higher level than in fact they possess. This section should also identify possible training needs, possible career development or promotion, pay, other benefits, any special aptitudes, for example, (manual dexterity to a particular level) to do the work.

The job analysis should also note the standard of behaviour or competency expected of staff. This will be an expression of how the successful candidate will use their skills, experience and knowledge, and how they will be manifested in their behaviour.

The methods by which the above information may be collected include:
- verbal assessment of the outgoing postholder
- exit interview
- a `will' on work in progress from the outgoing postholder
- postholder's comment on requirements in successor
- observing the job
- personnel or management documentation.

Stereotyping in recruitment

Perhaps the most substantial obstacle to fair and effective recruitment and selection is stereotyping. For most jobs, recruiters and indeed others will have a mental picture of what the person doing the job is like. This will not only include the relevant considerations of skills, abilities, experience and knowledge. It may also encompass age, gender - for example, secretaries are always women, engineers are always men - and race - NHS domestic staff in London are invariably female and of Afro-Caribbean origin, for instance. There are also, for most jobs, more subtle questions of dress and appearance - it is said that graphic designers never wear a suit - or values, often expressed through something as banal as the newspaper an individual reads - social workers always apparently read *The Guardian*.

Other areas where stereotypes might exist are in educational background, even in some instances down to specific universities or colleges, or social class. Educational background is, in reality, a covert method of establishing social class. Stereotypes might also encompass sexual orientation: male hairdressers are gay, for example. There will, of course, be individuals who fit in with the stereotypes. The danger resides in the belief that the stereotype is true in every case, even if it is true in some cases, or even in most.

The impact of this sometimes subtle, and sometimes clumsy interplay of prejudice and cliche is that when candidates present themselves who do not conform to the stereotype, they will have to work that much harder to be taken seriously, or in some instances, to even get a hearing. They thus not only have to prove their competence, but also their ability to do the job even though they are not like the others who currently do the job. They have to display their ability to fit in.

The corollary of this is that people who may comply with the stereotypes in gender, age, values and so on may, if they present themselves effectively and are not asked for an adequate demonstration of their skills, be appointed to jobs they cannot do. Most people will have encountered this kind of person some time in their working life and it will doubtless have caused them significant irritation.

Many recruiters are left sanguine by the essential irrationality of this approach. Research in particular by Meredith Belbin (*Management Teams: Why They Succeed or Fail*, 1981) and Tom Peters and Robert H. Waterman jnr (*In Search of Excellence*, 1981) has shown that successful teams will be built not on similarity, but on a diverse range of backgrounds, experiences and approaches and, in recruitment and selection, employers should be seeking to broaden the skills base of the existing workforce, not simply replicate its existing gaps.

Teams built on difference and diversity may of course present a greater management challenge but a quiet life for a manager is not, officially at least, a high priority in recruitment and selection.

If recruitment proceeds without thorough job analysis the danger of unchallenged stereotypes impacting on the recruitment is significantly increased. Without a clear framework of skills, experiences, competencies and knowledge being defined and sought recruiters will `default' to existing preconceptions and assumptions.

CHAPTER 5

JOB DESCRIPTIONS AND PERSON SPECIFICATIONS

Once the job analysis has been completed the manager of the post being recruited for and the personnel staff can set about putting the appropriate documentation in place for the recruitment, ie, the job description, the person specification and the advertisement.

Drafting a job description

Job descriptions fulfil the function of telling prospective and current postholders what the job involves. They are essential to effective recruitment and appraisal; and may also be used in the event of grievances, disputes or industrial tribunals. Descriptions should therefore be:
- accurate
- objective
- consistent
- measurable
- justifiable.

They should contain:
- objectives of the post
- areas of responsibility

54   Fair Recruitment and Selection

- regular and irregular duties
- people that the postholder is responsible to
- people that the postholder is responsible for
- standards of expected performance and competency.

Drafting a person specification

The person specification indicates what criteria the candidates have to meet to be considered for the job and should be based as closely as possible on the job description. It should express the requirements of the job in terms of the person being sought: the skills and abilities, the knowledge, experience and other qualities being sought in suitable candidates. Depending on the job, there may well be others. For example, there may be a section on personal qualities. Whilst personal qualities clearly do affect the ability of an individual to do the job, they should not be seen as substitutes for skills. An instance would be that dealing with irate customers is a skill. Simply possessing the personal quality of patience will not be enough.

The criteria on the person specification are often listed according to whether they are essential or desirable. It is perhaps more helpful to rank the quality sought, or weight them out of 100 per cent, so that recruiters have clearly identified what are the most important qualities that the successful candidate must have.

If candidates are not expected to possess all the necessary skills on joining and training is offered then this should also be noted on the person specification.

Person specification checklist

The following key points should be borne in mind when drawing up a person specification.

1) Subjective or ambiguous criteria, which are matters of judgement and for which little evidence can be found in the recruitment process, should be avoided, for example: 'working in a team'; 'self-starter'; 'motivated'; 'flexible'; or 'good with people'.

2) The standards required should be described specifically. For example,
   don't say: 'Good inter-personal skills';
   do say: 'Ability to negotiate compromises and resolve conflict between staff amicably'; 'Courteous with all customers, both internal and external'; 'Clear, concise verbal communication'.

3) All criteria should be job-related.

4) Skills and abilities should be emphasized. Education and experience are often used as a shorthand for skills and abilities, and can be misleading. It is perfectly possible to acquire a qualification in a subject, without acquiring the skill to do it, for example, a language qualification does not necessarily imply the ability either to speak or to write in that language. The qualification may also have been gained a long time ago. On the other hand, many people will have gained skills through experience, either at work, or, in some instances, outside work.

   Experience is however not in itself evidence of a skill. It may be that a candidate has got experience of having done something badly! Alternatively, they may have experience of doing a small number of tasks and responsibilities over and over again. So, although they may have ten years of experience, the skills and abilities learnt in that time in fact only took a year.

56   Fair Recruitment and Selection

5) The minimum length of experience should be stated. Longer experience does not always means greater skills. The quality of the experience should also be stated. Defining the relevant level of experience involves answering the questions: what has the candidate have to have done, for how long, and to what standard?

6) Abilities should be expressed in terms of the standards required, not just in terms of the task undertaken. For example,
don't say: 'Ability to write reports';
do say: 'Ability to write detailed reports on tenants' arrears for committees, including calculation of arrears, commentary and suggested legal or other action where appropriate'.

7) All recruiters should have the same interpretation of the criteria and know what they are looking for. This means that they have a shared understanding about the standards that the candidate will have to achieve in all the specified areas in order fully to meet the requirements of the job. See model person specification in appendix A 1.

CHAPTER 6

ATTRACTING A FIELD OF CANDIDATES

After the job description and the person specification have been prepared on the basis of the job analysis and the manager, the personnel staff and the other people involved in recruitment have agreed and understood the contents of these documents, the organization is then in a position to seek a field of suitable candidates.

In establishing a field of candidates, the recruiter's objectives are to attract the most suitable people for the job. The field may comprise only one person or it may be hundreds. How to establish the field will depend on what the recruiter thinks are the best ways of getting the right number of candidates and candidates with the right skills, qualifications and experience.

Aside from considerations of discrimination or unfairness, the choice of media will be affected by a number of other factors. These include: cost, timescale, maximising the number of suitable candidates and minimising the number of unsuitable applicants.

Internal versus external advertising

The best way of getting a diverse field of suitable candidates is to advertise all posts internally and externally simultaneously so that candidates from within the organization have a chance equal to those from outside. This may, however, prove costly, both in time and money. There may be circumstances therefore where recruitment takes place from within the organization only.

If the existing workforce is unrepresentative, internal-only advertising is likely to perpetuate the current patterns and exclusion of those still outside the organization. In terms of fair recruitment and selection, therefore, internal-only advertising can be justified only where the existing workforce is diverse and representative, or where there are pressing operational reasons of time or money which make external advertising impractical.

Apart from the pragmatic justifications of time and money, the only other circumstances when, from the point of view of good practice the employer wants to recruit internally only is where the intention is to give career development opportunities to existing staff. Career development should not mean automatic promotion after a certain period, even when there are more able candidates outside the organization. The employer's responsibility is to ensure that their staff get the training and development to compete equally with outsiders for more complex and senior jobs than the ones they do at the moment.

Internal-only advertising should therefore solely be used to encourage career development where there is an internal field of suitably skilled, trained candidates, which is also representative in terms of race and gender.

Discriminatory practice: word of mouth

Recruitment by word of mouth is obviously very restrictive and is unlikely to extend the range and network of people employed by the organization. It is not therefore recommended in the context of recruiting for diversity. The same applies to recruitment at the gatepost, as this also requires previous 'inside information'.

Institutions, schemes, agencies and media

Schools and colleges

Potential sources of candidates for posts include schools and colleges. These will obviously be most appropriate where the job does not require previous work experience. In order to be fair, the recruiters should avoid only choosing schools of a type or in areas where there are not significant numbers of ethnic minority pupils. So, for example, choosing a school in rural Cheshire to recruit for a job in central Manchester will almost certainly produce a field of candidates skewed towards white people and unrepresentative of the population of the city. Alternatively, recruiting solely from an independent school and not seeking candidates from local state or grant-maintained schools is also likely to produce an unrepresentative field.

Training schemes

Training schemes are also a source of candidates. Again they will be suitable when no previous permanent work experience is needed, although many training schemes now include a period of work experience. The points mentioned above about the location and type of training

Positive action training schemes

As already discussed, both the Race Relations Act 1976 and the Sex Discrimination Act 1975 permit positive action in training. There are a number of training schemes targeted specifically at black and ethnic minority people and woman for jobs, or in areas, where those groups are under-represented in the existing workforce. An organization which is keen to avoid bias, and to attract the widest range of suitably qualified candidates may specifically seek out these positive action training schemes and recruit from them.

Employers may also run their own positive action training schemes. In order to do this they have to ensure that the group being targeted is under-represented. They can design a training programme and advertise it solely for members of the targeted group. If the training is satisfactorily completed, the organization cannot simply slot the person into a permanent, non-trainee post. They must compete. There can be no discrimination at the point of selection, only in helping people from under-represented groups to prepare to compete.

These positive action training schemes are most appropriate if there is not a field of suitably qualified candidates, either within the organization, or outside it, from the targeted group. If there is a group of suitably qualified people of all backgrounds in the market, the aim of the recruitment process is to identify them and to encourage them to apply. Training is not a substitute for failure to reach suitably qualified candidates as it gives the unwelcome message that white people and men can come straight in and do the job whereas black people or women require special help. Where that message is given out, it has, at least, to be true in those cases.

Job centres

People who are unemployed and available for work are required to register with job centres. Recruiting from job centres is therefore a good way of attracting a wide range of candidates. Many recruiters are unjustly and unjustifiably biased against people who are unemployed. They are believed to be less able than people currently in work. There is often a vague suspicion, which is sometimes quite explicit, that they brought unemployment on themselves through incompetence, being work-shy, or some other personal inadequacy. There is no evidence for these views and indeed in the future more and more people, perhaps most people, will have periods of unemployment or under-employment during their careers.

It is also worth noting that black and ethnic minority people and people with disabilities are over-represented amongst unemployed people, and so any recruitment strategy that is biased against that group may also indirectly discriminate on the grounds of race or disability.

University appointment boards

These are obviously a good source of graduate applicants. Organizations need however to be sure that education up to graduate level is really required for the post. For some jobs, for example, in engineering or chemistry, this will be obvious. For others, though, organizations have a misplaced and unjustified faith in the virtues of intellect and youth, even supposing that these virtues are always present in graduates. Again black and ethnic minority people are still proportionately under-represented amongst graduates, so where degrees are sought unnecessarily, they are likely to be unfairly excluded.

Agencies and consultants

The use of employment agencies and consultants is often a way of reducing the amount of work that the organization needs to do in recruitment. However, the recruiting organization will need to be sure firstly that the agency is fully briefed on their specific requirements. The job of secretary, for example, is by no means the same in every organization. Also, the employer will want to ensure that the agency does not discriminate on its behalf. It is of course unlawful for a recruiting organization to give instructions to an agency to discriminate on its behalf on the grounds of race or gender, although there are other types of unfair discrimination, for instance, exclusion on the grounds of age, which are not likely to be a breach of the legislation.

In some instances, agencies will make assumptions without instructions about the suitability of certain age groups, or racial groups. Organizations need therefore to make it clear to agencies that they do not wish to specify the age, gender or racial origin of the candidates, and they do not want the agency to do so on their behalf. It is good practice to give the agency a copy of the organization's equal opportunities policy with a covering letter explaining the above.

Recruitment consultants have multiplied in recent years, particularly for more senior and executive jobs. Organizations, again, will want to ensure that they do not discriminate on their behalf. They will also want to be sure that the consultant does not simply use their own personal network to establish a shortlist. There will be few consultants who really do know personally all the suitably qualified candidates for a post, so it is important to insist on a wider, more open trawl of the market for a particular job through advertising or by some other means. Personal networks in recruitment tend, perhaps not surprisingly, to produce successful candidates who bear a remarkable resemblance in background, age, racial origin and gender to the person doing the searching.

Newspapers and journals

Advertisements in local and national newspapers and trade journals are a popular source of recruitment. Recruiting organizations will want to make sure that the choice of local newspaper does not exclude certain racial groups because of the local population in their area of circulation. Using journals also may exclude other groups. For example, advertising for care staff in women's magazines is unlikely to produce suitably qualified male candidates. Trade journals should be used where it is likely that all the suitably qualified candidates are likely to have access to that journal. It would, for example, be unwise to advertise a job for a book-keeper in a journal targeted specifically at qualified accountants. Also, people outside the trade who are suitably qualified may not see the advertisement. So, for example, to advertise a finance job in a housing journal just because the organization is a housing organization is likely to exclude many suitably qualified candidates who do not currently work in housing.

There are also an increasing number of black and ethnic minority newspapers and journals; publications specifically aimed at women; or people with disabilities; or aimed at gay men and lesbians. These are obviously a good place to widen the network of people seeing the advertisement and responding to it. Advertising in targeted papers also sends out a positive message about the organization's commitment to equality of opportunity and recruiting for diversity.

Information to inquirers

The information that is sent to people expressing an interest in the job is crucial to their decision about whether or not to apply. They will need:

1) a more detailed description of the organization;
2) information about the work of the department they may be joining;
3) the job description and possibly the person specification;
4) information about the organization's equal opportunities policy;
5) information about the organization's attitude to staff development;
6) guidance on the recruitment process, for example, whether particular information should be provided on the application form; any other tests or assessments they will be asked to undertake; the timescale for making the appointment.

Without a good information pack candidates will be `stabbing in the dark' and may not provide the necessary details for an effective recruitment decision.

Application forms

The application form is a key document for weeding out unsuitable candidates and identifying those who should go to the next stage. Many application forms contain a good deal of extraneous information and often do not elicit from the candidate the relevance of their previous experience and skills to the job for which they now wish to be considered.

Irrelevant information that should not be sought on application forms include: age; marital status; number of children; nationality (except where a work permit might be needed); schools attended (as opposed to qualifications achieved).

Even if irrelevant information is not specifically sought, it will sometimes be provided by the candidate unsolicited. There is no foolproof way of screening out irrelevant information, or information that would allow recruiters to identify ethnic origin or age. For example, overseas qualifications will give an indication of ethnic origin, just as dates when qualifications were achieved will give an indication of age. There is little point therefore in seeking ever more obtuse ways to restrict recruiters. Recruiters must be trained, and impose a degree of integrity and self-discipline on themselves, such that if they do think they know a candidate's ethnic origin or age, it does not mar or cloud their judgement about skills, knowledge or experience. An example of an application form is given in appendix A 2.

Organizations may very well wish to monitor the age, gender, disability or ethnic origin of people applying for posts with the organization. This is covered in more detail in chapter 12. The information should not however be accessible to recruiters.

Curricula vitae

It is increasingly common for individuals seeking employment to have prepared a curriculum vitae (cv). This saves employers the bother of devising a suitable application form. There are however dangers. The information given may contain a good deal of irrelevant material which will get in the way of objective decision-making. Secondly, the material on the cv may not address the specific requirements of the job in hand. Some organizations now, therefore, refuse to accept cvs at all. This may be going a bit far. Where cvs are accepted, it is good practice to ask candidates to fill in a cover sheet which asks them to specifically address the requirements of the job and to match their past experience, knowledge and skills to the job under consideration. An example of such a cover sheet is given in appendix A 3.

CHAPTER 7

JOB ADVERTSING

Although the main purpose of a job advertisement is obviously to produce a field of candidates, there are subsidiary purposes which include:

1) minimising the number of unsuitable applicants;
2) facilitating future job recruitment - research evidence suggests that people take into account both current advertisements and previous ones in deciding whether or not to apply for a job;
3) enhancing the public reputation of the recruiting organization.

Most would-be candidates look for the following information in an advertisement:

1) the job to be done
2) its location
3) remuneration offered
4) type of person required
5) factors that might mean they would not be considered
6) indications about whether or not they are likely to be successful.

A good advertisement will therefore provide information about:

- the company or organization
- the post
- the remuneration
- the sort of person that will be successful.

Advertisements which deter applications

Advertisements are also the stage in the recruitment process where most people exclude themselves from consideration. Some of them do so because they think that they are not right for the job or that the job or organization is not right for them. But what is this opinion based on?

Sometimes it is founded on the image of the job or the organization. The applicant may have a preconceived notion about the organization and the type of people who work there. This explains why, despite over a decade of advertisements that contain the words 'equal opportunity employer', the mix of applicants by gender and race has remained the same in many organizations.

For instance, a black applicant may be aware that the organization has few black employees and may believe that it is not interested in hiring black people. On the other hand, a woman might see a job advertised and fail to apply for it because she perceived the work or the culture of the organization as being too male. Job advertising can be used to overcome these preconceptions and encourage qualified members of under-represented groups to apply by letting them know that they are welcome and that they will be treated fairly.

In many cases, the contents of the advertisement itself may deter qualified candidates from applying. The advertisement's text and images may imply that only one group of people will be considered for employment.

For instance, an advertisement headed 'pest control men' even if it contains the words, 'we are an equal opportunity employer' in the text, implies that only men will be considered. Similarly, an advertisement for a manager that has an illustration of a white man may give applicants the message that the company is seeking only people of this sex and race. Women and black people may therefore not apply, even though they are qualified.

Another deterrent factor may be the paper or journal in which the advertisement is printed. If an advertisement is placed in a journal which is perceived as targeting a particular group, people who are not members of that group will either not see the advertisement, or else will infer that they need not apply because they are not part of the targeted group.

Equal opportunities statements

It has become increasingly common to see the statement, `we are an equal opportunities employer' or, 'working towards equal opportunities' on advertisements. This practice is to be encouraged, however it is now seen so frequently that the impact has been significantly reduced. Organizations which want to target under-represented groups through their advertisements will have to do a good deal more. Guidance on this issue is given below.

Targeted advertising

Just as job advertising may be a deterrent to applicants, it can also be used to attract a particular applicant pool. This is known as targeted recruitment. It is lawful so long as it is done in a non-discriminatory way.

To avoid discrimination, the employer must first

establish if the group to be targeted is under-represented in the workforce. The law makes a distinction about what this means for sex on the one hand and race on the other. As the law stands for men and women under-representation can be in a particular job across the country. With regard to race, under-representation is more narrowly defined, referring to a particular job in a particular company or organization. If there is under-representation, then positive encouragement to apply can be given in the advertisements. However selection must remain non-discriminatory. This means that everyone must be judged for selection according to the same standards.

Targeted advertisements have been found to be most effective when they are carefully planned and have the co-operation of the workforce and the recruiters. The advertisements themselves should be catchy, with bold images and headlines that will attract members of the targeted group. At the same time, the advertisement should not discourage non-targeted applicant groups from applying. To do so would not only be counter-productive but also might be discriminatory.

To target a particular group, the following should be included in the advertisement:

1 a clear explanation of why the advertisement is being directed at a certain group;

2) a statement that the targeted group is encouraged to apply;

3) an indication that the organization or job is suitable for them no matter what they might have thought before;

4) a message that members of both sexes and all races are encouraged to apply. In addition to a statement to that effect, images should, where possible, show members of both sexes, and the wording should not

be couched entirely in terms of one sex or the other. Using the pronouns he and his or she and hers exclusively in the advertisement should be avoided. They can be left out altogether so that the advertisement is gender neutral. Alternatively, the plural form could be used. Whilst the use of they and them is not strictly grammatically correct, it will be widely understood, and not have the effect of putting off one or other gender;

5) a message to other potential candidates that their application will continue to be welcomed;

6) an assurance that selection will take place on a non-discriminatory basis.

Action taken by Rank Xerox provides a practical example of implementing this strategy. The company had found that men were under-represented in the position of customer response controllers. It therefore targeted men using an advertisement that conformed to the standards set out above. The headline was: 'Why are good men so difficult to find?' The text then set out Xerox's difficulties. They wanted to attract both men and women but few men applied.

The advertisement went on to discuss the problem in a balanced way, describing the job and setting out the requirements necessary for the successful applicant. It ended with the statement: 'Of course, although we're now looking for applications from men, we're still as keen as ever to hear from equally qualified women.' The photograph accompanying the advertisement showed two people at work as customer response controllers, one male, the other female. The advertisement was a success - not only did it produce more applications from men but also more from women.

Where the advertisement appears is almost as important as what is said in it. Putting an advertisement in the wrong place may mean that it does not reach all the potentially suitable applicants. For instance, if the workforce is almost exclusively male and the post is advertised only on workplace noticeboards, it is not only not reaching female applicants, but the organization may also find it is accused of unlawful indirect discrimination.

Job advertisers should consider the following questions:
– where should this post be advertised?
– what type of person is most likely to read the advertisement?
– where could the post be advertised so that it would reach the targeted group more effectively?

While targeted advertising is effective, it is not an overnight or total solution to all the problems of recruiting groups that are traditionally under-represented in certain jobs. In some cases, there may simply be very few qualified applicants from those groups. But advertising can be an important step in changing that. It gives a signal to careers officers, schools, students and parents that jobs previously seen as restricted to one sex or race are in fact open to all.

Rank Xerox, for example, had found that women were severely under-represented as customer engineers. Of 1,600 customer engineers, only 0.5 per cent were women. To redress this imbalance, they decided to target women when advertising for customer engineers.

The advertisements were headed: 'Is there one good reason why more customer engineers aren't women?" and showed a photograph of a female customer engineer at work. The text explained the problem, described the position and the qualifications required and emphasized that applications from both men and women were welcome. Nevertheless, very few women applied. Of 400 applicants, only 30 were women. Normally, however, advertisements for customer engineers received 175 responses, all from men. Few of the women who answered the advertisement had the skills or qualifications needed to do the job, and although one was offered the position, she did not take it.

Despite the small number of women who applied and the fact that none were actually appointed, the company felt that the advertisement had been a success. Male applicants had not been deterred and the advertisement had raised the profile of the company and sent a message to young women that the job of customer engineer was open to them.

Advertising for members of a particular race or sex

In some cases, advertisements indicate a requirement for a person of a specific race, national or ethnic origin, or gender. In these cases, there is a genuine occupational qualification for the postholder to be of a certain race or sex and the advertisement may specify that without being unlawful (see chapter 2).

Even in this case, the advertiser must be sure that the advertisement is not discriminatory. First, the job description must be checked to ensure that being of a particular race really is a genuine occupational qualification. If it is on the grounds of personal services that can best be delivered by a person of a particular racial or ethnic group, or gender, the services must be delivered on a face-to-face basis. Managerial posts do not generally qualify, unless the manager provides such personal services at least part of the time. Secondly, a description of these services should be included in the advertisement. Thirdly, the reason that these services can best be provided by a person of a particular sex or racial or ethnic group must be given. Fourthly, reference should be made to section 5 of the Race Relations Act or section 7 of the Sex Discrimination Act, which permit otherwise discriminatory acts on grounds of genuine occupational qualifications. Finally, since in this instance not all groups will be accepted for consideration, the usual equal opportunities statement should not be included in the advertisement.

Advertising for people with disabilities

People with disabilities have also been successfully targeted by using advertisements. During 1989, Channel 4 ran a campaign of advertisements titled: 'Disabled not Disqualified.' The text of the advertisement outlined two possible entry routes for people with disabilities. The first was to apply for one of a variety of jobs at their head office in London; the other was to apply for a place on a two-year training course. The advertisement ended with two messages: that disabled applicants would be welcomed and that the company was an equal opportunities employer. During a nine-month campaign, 280 people with disabilities were successfully attracted to apply.

Advertising through community networks

There are now many networks of organizations who work with people with disabilities, or with black and ethnic minority people. They will often have newsletters or information sheets, and are therefore a good low-cost addition to the circulation list for job advertisements. There is also the additional benefit that the organization is raising its profile in communities or amongst groups in society who may not know the organization exists at all, or may see it as a `white' or a `male' organization.

CHAPTER 8

SHORTLISTING

Who should shortlist?

Once applications have been received the next stage is to establish the shortlist. This should ideally be done at a meeting of all the people who will be involved in the interviewing or assessment process - the line manager, a personnel or human resources representative and someone with technical knowledge of how the job is done.

Where there are very large numbers of applicants it may not be practical to shortlist jointly. However, sending a list of names of possible interview candidates to the other interviewers is obviously prone to bias and subjectivity, particularly where those lists do not give any reasons for shortlisting some and rejecting others.

Shortlisting should also not be done by just one person. This obviously significantly increases the chance of decisions being affected by subjective opinions.

Whether the shortlisting is done in a group or alone, reasons for the shortlisting decision about each candidate should be recorded.

Length of shortlist

It is not advisable to decide on the maximum number of people to be shortlisted in advance. It is however advisable to decide on a minimum number. Any number smaller than four is unlikely to give an adequate basis of comparison; shortlists of one are never desirable.

The first task is to establish whom amongst the applicants meets the person specification. If there is a sufficient number the recruiters will have to go no further in establishing the shortlist. If there are not enough, it is best either to re-advertise or reconsider whether everything on the person specification is essential. The danger of discrimination lies in taking the candidate who is 'nearest' to meeting the person specification. This undermines the objectivity of the process and calls into question the basis on which the person specification was originally decided.

The person specification should not be so drastically altered that the job is no longer the one that was originally advertised. People who thought they were not eligible but who, according to the revised person specification, may well be, will thereby have been unfairly excluded. If marginal revisions are made to the person specification, all candidates who meet the revised requirements should be seen.

Shortlisting techniques

A job-related skills test may also be used to sift out unsuitable applicants. This type of test has the added advantage of helping the recruiters find out in an objective way which applicants can do the job.

Some organizations employ two filtering mechanisms, for example, to help in selection. For certain jobs, a sheet of supplementary questions is included with the application form. Correct answers must be given if the applicant is to proceed to the next stage.

Where supplementary questions are to be included with the job application, they should be pertinent to the post. For instance, it would be reasonable to ask candidates for a computer job about software and systems experience, but not about British history which has no relevance to the job.

Another method of filtering is to ask applicants to give an oral or written presentation. This may be a good test of skills for some posts, for example, a position in the personnel department. Here, applicants could be asked to prepare a ten-minute presentation on one of several topics. This would enable the interview panel to judge the candidates' skills more accurately.

Requesting presentations for jobs in which presentations never or rarely have to be given, is not a good idea. It creates a bias towards the smooth and articulate. These are often deceptive qualities, suggesting a level of competence that is not always present.

Filtering mechanisms such as these may, however, result in unfair treatment if not properly used. For example, if an advertisement asked applicants to telephone to discuss the job and answer questions before receiving an application form, people who stutter or have a hearing difficulty might be at a disadvantage. Where the job does not involve work on the telephone, employers should allow those individuals to apply in writing. If candidates are asked to ring in for more information, or to discuss the post, whether or not the telephone conversation forms part of the assessment should be made clear to them.

Such mechanisms may also result in standards being raised to a level not really necessary to do the job well. Many potential applicants might therefore be discouraged from applying or might not be considered even if they did apply. If many women or ethnic minority applicants were discouraged by raising standards for all applicants beyond what the job required, this would be a form of indirect discrimination and therefore possibly unlawful.

In choosing a shortlist from a large number of applicants care must be taken, both to conform with the law against direct and indirect discrimination and to avoid sifting out qualified applicants by introducing unreasonable selection procedures.

Where hundreds or even thousands of applications are received as a result of an advertisement, sometimes the only fair method of shortlisting is very labour intensive. For example, when the Staffordshire fire service advertised 20 vacancies, 5,000 replies were received. Making the shortlist took three officers nine days. Each application was read, carefully considered, and coded so that the fire service could look back and see why an applicant had not been selected.

The number of applicants was reduced at the outset by rejecting anyone who did not apply by a certain date, or return the form by a certain date, or enclose a stamped self-addressed envelope. Successful applicants were given three month's notice of a series of dates on which they would be tested physically and mentally. Anyone who could not attend was also excluded.

Although the Staffordshire fire service was dismayed by the large number of applicants, it has remained determined to encourage applications from qualified ethnic minority candidates and women who are under-represented in the fire service. Application forms have been redesigned so that computers can be used to sift through applications more quickly. (See also the specimen shortlisting form in appendix A 4).

Where there are too many people who meet the person specification to take to the next stage of the recruitment process a sifting mechanism will have to be established. As shown in the above example, this should not be simply to raise the standards required for the job above what is actually required until only a small number of people meet them. This will discriminate against people who may lack formal qualifications or extensive experience but who are quite capable of doing the job.

There are various more equitable ways of sifting out. For instance in addition to the methods already illustrated, the candidates who have special skills which may not be essential for the job but which would be useful in the job or would add to the collection of skills in the team or department can be considered. An example of this would be second language skills or knowledge of a particular culture from which the organization has many clients.

Alternatively, a short preliminary interview for all candidates who meet the person specification could be arranged; or they could be given an aptitude or skills test based on the job, which would then be used to establish a more manageable shortlist.

Random selection even amongst those who meet the person specification is not a satisfactory shortlisting mechanism because it may result in the best candidates being randomly rejected. There are few posts for which job-related tests cannot be devised to reduce the number of candidates to be considered to a manageable number.

The next section discusses planning and running an assessment centre, exploring in more detail job-related tests and how they can be used for shortlisting.

Planning and running assessment centres

An assessment centre is a series of tests given to a group of candidates who are observed by a team of assessors. The tests and exercises are designed to predict how well they will do the job. Job simulation exercises make up the bulk of the tests but standardized tests such as intelligence or personality tests may also be included.

Conducted properly an assessment centre can be the fairest and most objective way of assessing applicants. The tests and exercises can be chosen on the basis of the skills and abilities that the job requires using the person specification. They can then reveal the skills the applicants already possess, as well as their potential for development. The use of a number of different tests can allow the employer to gain a more complete picture of the way a prospective employee should perform. For those who have no previous permanent work record, such as school leavers and graduates, assessment centres can be an invaluable selection tool.

If an assessment centre is conducted improperly, however, either in the type of tests chosen or the way in which the candidates are assessed, the wrong people will be chosen for the job. Discrimination may also occur. Where candidates from certain groups do poorly compared to those from other groups, the employer may be responsible for an act of indirect discrimination. The key to avoiding discriminatory practices is to be sure that the tests are correctly designed and administered and that they are free of bias.

Although assessment centres offer the promise of objectivity, since all of the candidates take the same tests and are judged according to the same standards, long-standing racial and sex discrimination in society may mean that everyone does not have an equal chance. Some tests may be culturally biased, meaning that people from one culture or of one sex do better in them. And even if the tests and exercises are fair, the assessors may be biased against candidates from certain groups, and so assess individuals from those groups more harshly or using different standards.

To be sure that the assessment centre is both efficient and non-discriminatory, exercises should be chosen that test the skills needed to do the job and that can be evaluated objectively. Assessors will need training in how to conduct the tests and assess applicants. Finally, tests should be monitored to ensure that they are a valid way of assessing applicants: did the applicants selected do as well in the post as the tests predicted?

Choosing the right tests

The first step in choosing the right test is to look at the person specification to see what skills and aptitudes are needed to do the job well. For instance, does the job require the applicant to be able to work as part of a group? Then an exercise involving teamwork would be useful in assessing those skills.

If the tests are chosen without reference to the person specification, they are neither valid nor cost-effective since they do not show who can best fill the post. They might also cause indirect discrimination. A report-writing exercise, for example, might be appropriate in some cases (if writing reports is part of the job description), but if the ability to write English fluently

82 Fair Recruitment and Selection

is not part of the job, a writing test might be a form of indirect discrimination against people whose first language is not English.

Where the post could be filled by a person with a disability, the test conditions should not put people with disabilities at a disadvantage. If a postholder with a disability would be provided with adaptations to help him or her do the job, any applicants with disabilities should be allowed to use similar adaptations as necessary during the test. For example, a person with dyslexia might be allowed to do the written exercises on a computer with a spell-check facility.

Assessment centres normally use a combination of standardized tests such as tests of skills, aptitudes, intelligence, interests and personality as well as job simulation exercises. Choosing the right standardized psychometric tests requires care if discrimination is to be avoided. The next part of this chapter explains how to vet such tests to be sure that they do not lead to discrimination against particular groups of applicants.

Avoiding discriminatory tests

In order to avoid the possibility of indirect discrimination as well as to be sure that the assessment centre is efficient and effective, the following questions need to be asked when choosing tests and exercises:

1) Is this test or exercise genuinely relevant to the assessment of the skills needed for this job?
2) Does the test reliably identify the skills or qualities that are being sought?
3) Does the test give consistent results every time it is administered?
4) Will the test seem appropriate to the candidates who are taking it? If not, they may lose confidence

in the ability of the assessment centre to judge their skills fairly.

5) Have other employers, who are using the test for a similar purpose, found it to be effective?

6) Are the norms, or scoring patterns, used for a standardized test up-to-date? Scoring patterns change over time and out-of-date norms can invalidate the test results. Also, were the norms created using a test group that contained women and a representative sample of different racial and cultural groups? If not, the test may not provide a valid picture of an applicants' skills.

7) Does the test discriminate unfairly against any particular group? While it may not be possible to create a completely bias-free test, it is possible to take any bias into account in evaluating the results.

8) Will current members of staff require any special training to administer the test?

If a standardized test is going to be used, the test manufacturer should be able to answer these questions. The British Psychological Society and the Institute of Personnel Management may also be able to give help or advice on how to choose a test. If the answer to any of the questions is not satisfactory, the test in the assessment centre should not be included.

Job simulations tests, not standardized tests, however form the core of an assessment centre. When choosing or creating job simulation tests, it is vital to ensure that they test the skills and competencies needed to do the job. The more closely they are related to job performance, the more useful they will be.

Simulation exercises may include group discussion, group problem solving, individual job simulation tasks, job-related role play, in-tray exercises, or written and oral presentations. The type and mixture of exercises

84 Fair Recruitment and Selection

should be directly related to the skills needed for the particular job. Such exercises are often designed by recruiters in-house. When designing them, there must be a realistic test of the skills needed for the job; the material used must be understandable by the target applicant pool; the time limit given must be realistic; and the exercises must be objectively assessable.

A working party consisting of several managers and a personnel officer should design exercises. The managers can provide ideas which the personnel officer can then write up into an exercise. After checking by the working party, the exercise should be tested both against the criteria listed above and on real people before being used in the assessment centre.

Observation sheets to be used by the assessors in rating the candidates should also be made up by the working party. These sheets should include a checklist of characteristics, qualities or skills that should be displayed in each exercise. For example, when rating participants in a group discussion, the qualities on the checklist might be: (1) originality; (2) relevance; (3) involvement; (4) pertinent comments; (5) influence over other group members; and (6) creativity. Some organizations hire an external assessor with special skills in occupational psychology or training to help assess candidates.

Weighting the tests

Another aspect of the assessment centre that requires careful consideration is how the tests should be weighted in relation to each other. Are they all of equal importance in the ability to do the job well, or are some skills or abilities more important than others? The competencies and qualities to be assessed ought to be listed and ranked in order of importance. Interviewers should then use this as a guide when making up a grading system. The most important skills should be given the greatest weight in the overall marking.

On the day, administration of the test must also be fair. The place where the test is to be held should be well-lit, kept at a comfortable temperature and free of unnecessary noise. The staff assessing the test should have received training both in how to assess the tests and exercises being given and in equal opportunities. They must be sure that they are not putting members of any one group at a disadvantage. For example, addressing female candidates as 'young lady' is both patronizing and off-putting and should be avoided.

An important part of non-discriminatory testing is making sure that all the candidates understand the test procedures. Assessors should not take any knowledge on the part of candidates for granted. The test rules and procedures should be explained both orally and in writing. Before beginning the test, the assessors should make sure that everyone has understood the instructions. For example, some candidates may not realize that they can go back over their work or skip a question that they do not know the answer to. If there are any time-limits on the test, the candidates should be told beforehand so that they can budget their time accordingly.

A brochure or sheet can be sent to the candidates well before the day of the assessment centre. It might include sample questions or exercises so that the candidates can familiarize themselves with any unfamiliar procedures. By knowing what to expect, candidates will be able to perform at their best and the assessor will be better able to judge their skills and abilities.

Results of the performance of individuals at the assessment centre are confidential. Assessors should not breach this confidentiality. The applicants are entitled to receive some kind of feedback on their performance on the tests. The same level of feedback should be offered to all applicants.

Evaluating an assessment centre

After setting up and running the assessment centre it should evaluated to find out if it was effective in selecting applicants and to be sure that it was not biased in any way. This information will be helpful the next time the organization runs an assessment centre.

Begin with the first impressions of the assessors. Were any of the tests difficult to rate or score? These may need to be reworked, or if that is not possible, omitted in future. Were there any tests on which all the applicants received equal scores? Such tests do not help to choose between the applicants and are therefore a waste of time. Another important question to ask is: was the assessment centre a cost-effective way to choose the best candidate?

If any test was biased against one particular group of candidates, it should not be used again. In the long term, records should be kept on the performance of candidates according to race and sex.

The most important measure of the success of an assessment centre is if the people recruited as a result perform as well at their jobs as the test indicated they would. If there is a discrepancy, the job description and the tests and exercises being used will have to be reviewed.

The results of an assessment centre can only be a guide to who should be employed. References and interviews should also be taken into account. It is therefore unwise to create cut-off points or scores below which applicants will not be considered. When scoring the tests and exercises, stick to the rules and standards that were set up initially. When used properly and fairly, an assessment centre may provide a great deal of information about a candidate's abilities and skills, and be of great value in appointing the right applicant.

CHAPTER 9

INTERVIEWING

Alongside other assessments based as closely as possible on the job itself, the interview is an important part of the recruitment process. Nonetheless, the interview may be an unreliable recruitment technique: it maximises the opportunity for stereotyping on the basis of appearance, accent or some other irrelevant, subjective consideration. Despite all this, it would be a brave recruiter who would employ somebody solely on the basis of performance in tests without meeting them. The structure of the interview and the questions which are asked will decide whether or not useful and relevant information is drawn out for the purpose of selection.

The interview may come after other job-related tests, or they may follow. Other assessment techniques are discussed in chapter 10.

Interview panel members

Interviews should not be conducted by one person alone. The opportunities for bias are considerable, and it is not the most effective way of getting the best from all candidates. On the other hand interviews by committees are extremely daunting and making decisions afterwards can be a difficult process. Messy `horse-trading' and airing vested interests unrelated to the merits of the candidates may be among the unwanted results.

The ideal number is three or four. This should include the line manager of the post, someone from personnel and someone with hands-on technical knowledge of the job. There may be others who also have a particular expertise which would be useful.

Preparing for interviews

Person specification

The interview panel should meet at least half an hour before the first interview. They should initially consider the original person specification. From this they should identify the key areas they want to assess in the interview. They should also decide what weight they attach to each quality. This can be done either by ranking them in priority order, or classing some as essential and some as desirable, or by splitting up 100 per cent between all the key areas. This list should be as complete as possible. It should take in technical as well as interpersonal areas.

Not all the key areas can be considered in an interview. Where technical competence needs to be evaluated, other tests will have to be devised, for example, an accountancy test. Hopefully these assessments or tests will have been devised when the person specification was drafted. Some of them may already have taken place, either as an aid to shortlisting, or in preparation for the interview.

For those areas which are going to be assessed in the interview, the interviewers must then decide what questions they are going to ask (see below).

Application forms

Interviewers should remind themselves about the contents of the application forms before the interviews begin. Agreement should be reached about what, if anything, on the application form needs clarifying by each candidate.

Decision-making process

An agreement should then be reached about how the decision to appoint is going to be made. Who will have the final say? Are there areas of technical competence which only some members of the interview panel are qualified to assess? If so, they should have the final say in these areas.

Environment

Surroundings are important in making candidates feel relaxed. The list below has the main suggestions of what might help:

1) have somewhere for candidates to leave their coats;
2) all the chairs should be at the same height and not too low - armchairs that are difficult to get in and out of are not relaxing
3) have a coffee table or somewhere for papers - a desk or a meeting table may be off-putting;
4) have a glass of water for candidates;
5) ask the receptionist to ensure that candidates are offered a cup of tea or coffee;
6) avoid very bright lights;

7) don't seat candidates facing windows with the light shining in their eyes.

Behaviour

Interviewers need to ensure that the words they are using are supported by their behaviour or non-verbal communication. It is important to maintain eye contact with the candidate, even when another member of the panel is doing the questioning. Tone and volume of voice also needs to be friendly but firm; similarly with facial expression. Gestures, such as fidgeting with jewellery, keys or pens will also need to be controlled, so as not to put off the candidate. Doodling should be avoided, unless absolutely compulsive. Posture should not be slouched as this will convey indifference. Lastly, the distance between the candidate and the panel should not be so great as to be remote and intimidating, and not so close as to be falsely intimate.

Creating rapport

Some recruiters appear to believe that the best approach to interviewing is to disconcert the interviewee as comprehensively as possible, and if they do not go to pieces, that is evidence of their suitability for the post. Whilst this might make the interviewer feel powerful it is unlikely to lead to good recruitment decisions.

To get the best from a candidate, interviewers should indicate that they have some empathy with the situation that the candidate is in, and that the interviewers also want them to perform well. A remark like, 'Take a moment to think about this before answering if you need to' will reassure candidates.

Openings

To begin with, sending out a member of the interview panel to fetch the candidate is a welcoming gesture. The opening stages of the interview are critical to putting candidates at their ease and thereby getting the best out of them. All the panel should stand up when the candidate enters and shake hands. A few pleasantries such as, `How was your journey?' will allow the candidate to speak in the room to the group and so judge the right volume for their voice, hear the voices of the panel and get over their initial nerves. Panel members should also introduce themselves, giving their name and a little information about what they do. The chair of the panel can then explain the structure of the interview, how long it will last, and whether there will be any other tests or assessments.

Candidates should also be told about the arrangements for note-taking as this may put them off. Notes taken in interviews are essential aide-memoires. It will help to put candidates at their ease if they are told that notes will be taken to assist in remembering what a candidate said. As eye contact is important, interviewers should try not to take notes while a candidate is speaking directly to them. It is less intrusive to write notes once another member of the panel has taken up the questioning. Interviewers should however take care to record what a candidate said, or some abbreviation of it, not their opinion of what the person said. A note such as, `Not very good answer' will not assist in remembering what a candidate said after a long day's interviewing. It is also often possible for candidates to read what is being written and an indiscreet note could be extremely off-putting.

Interview questioning

There is a popularly held misconception that the way to ensure equal opportunities during interviews is to ask all candidates exactly the same questions. This does not work. Questions that are too formal merely serve to make candidates feel ill at ease. Uniform questioning does not enable the interviewer to draw out particular candidates on a subject that they may not have covered well, and does not give candidates a chance to add anything that they may have forgotten when they first answered the question.

What is imperative in ensuring equal opportunities is that the same ground is covered with all candidates so that they all have an equal chance of showing their skills to the best advantage. Also, the ground covered should all be relevant. The danger is that stereotypes may be brought into play in leading questions which undermine a particular candidate's chances of success. An example of this would be asking a young woman candidate whether she is intending to get married and have children.

Once having decided upon the content of the questions, interviewers can then decide about who is going to ask which ones.

First question

The first question should allow the candidate an opportunity to talk about themselves and their past experience in the way they think appropriate. So the opening question could ask them to relate their previous experience to this job. This information should give the interviewers plenty of material with which to work later in the interview.

94 Fair Recruitment and Selection

After the candidates have had the chance to talk about themselves and their experience, skills and knowledge the questioning can then move onto issues that arise out of the application form or the cv. These questions should ideally be asked by the manager or the person who has the final say on the appointment. In preparing for an interview the panel should agree the aspects about which more information will be sought from each candidate. Interviewers should not cross-examine the candidate for the `true meaning' of what they have said: the focus should be on seeking clarification or further details. Having established the matters of fact, the panel can then use the rest of the interview to ask more analytical questions.

Open questions

Such questions provide a framework for the respondent in terms of subject matter, but they impose no constraints on the time a person takes to answer the question or the information they volunteer in answering the question. Wherever possible, this type of question should be used during interviews for opening up discussion of the criteria on the person specification and whether or not candidates meet them. It is quite rare for open questions to be biased or prejudiced.

Follow-up questions

Once a candidate has answered an open question, the interviewer may want to ask a follow-up question to clarify what they have said, or to probe more deeply, or to seek examples about when they have had to demonstrate the skills, or experience they have described. Follow-up questions are critical to assessment but they do contain risks. It is in asking follow-up questions that there is the greatest temptation to ask leading questions, or to imply an answer in the way that the question is asked: `So you would say you could do that, then?' A candidate is hardly likely to say No!

Closed questions

Questions such as these seek factual information. For example, 'When will you be able to start?' is a closed but objective question.

Leading questions

These are the sort of questions that are most often biased or prejudiced. They usually require the answer Yes or No, and may be loaded. The right answer is often implied by the way that the question is asked. For example, 'And you left in September?' is a leading question but it implies no value judgement about the fact that the person left in September.

On the other hand if the question was phrased, 'And then you left in September to have a baby and you did not return to work for two years?' it would clearly be a loaded question. It implies a judgement, possibly disapproval, and suggests assumptions about why the woman stayed at home for two years.

She may not have stayed at home to look after the baby. She may have been ill, or not got a job for any number of reasons, most of which are not likely to be anything to do with her ability to do the job she is applying for.

In general, leading questions should be avoided, but where they are used care should be taken to ensure that they are not loaded with a particular assumption; do not

96 Fair Recruitment and Selection

make irrelevant value judgements; and do not form the impression in the candidate's mind that information is being sought which will subsequently be used to discriminate against them.

`How-to' questions

Asking candidates how they would handle a real-life situation will often be helpful, particularly if it is an area where they have previous experience. Asking inexperienced candidates will not tell the recruiters very much. What people say they would do and what they do in the event are inevitably often rather different, and this should be borne in mind in evaluating the answers to hypothetical questions.

If such a hypothetical question is asked and there is, in fact, no right or wrong answer, it is helpful to the candidate to tell them that.

Equal opportunities questions

Asking a question about equal opportunities at the interview is an increasingly standard feature. However many of the questions asked can be over-simplistic and tell the interviewers nothing of any importance. In asking an equal opportunities question the interviewers are seeking to establish two facts. First, does the candidate have unacceptable attitudes or beliefs which would prevent them from effectively performing all aspects of the job. Secondly, does the candidate have attitudes or beliefs which would prevent them from complying with the organization's equal opportunities commitments.

The best way to establish this is either by posing a case study or asking a hypothetical question. A common scenario at work could be described and the candidate then asked to consider how they would respond. It is best to avoid words which might be thought of as jargon, such as `racial harassment', `homophobia', `heterosexism' and so on.

As an illustration, one question could be: `A female member of staff is being persistently asked to go out for a drink with a male member of staff. She is not interested. You are her manager and she has complained to you. How would you respond?'

Another question might be, `A speaker on a training course persistently calls the women in the room "girls." You are one of the few male participants. It is suggested that you should have a word with him. What would you say?' This can be followed up by asking for examples of circumstances where candidates have had to handle similar issues.

An alternative sort of question would be based on experience. For example, `Have you had any experience of dealing with the needs of people who do not speak English?'

Bias in questions

Questions which lead to bias are those where an assumption is made about a particular candidate without that assumption being checked with the candidate for its veracity. So, for example, if a young Asian woman who is applying for a job working in pop music is asked if she is allowed to listen to pop music at home, assumptions are clearly being made about what goes on in Asian homes and the relationship between Asian young people and their parents.

Whilst the interviewer may have a belief that in general their view is correct, and indeed may have some evidence to support it, they are almost certain not to know the circumstances in which the candidate lives and are not therefore at liberty to ask questions as if something which may or may not be true in general is true in this case.

The candidate may of course deny the assumption that the interviewer has made and set the record straight. However such a line of questioning indicates prejudice working below the surface of the question and is also likely to have an unsettling effect on the candidate ensuring that they do not give of their best.

Listening skills

One of the common pitfalls amongst interviewers is to confuse what they have heard with what they have inferred from what was said, together with what they have simply assumed, whether or not the candidate had said something to give that impression.

Listening skills are required to ensure that interviewers accurately receive all the information and messages that a candidate gives, including non-verbal messages. The ability is needed to observe and to interpret as well as simply to hear. In interpreting what people say, interviewers should always note the evidence for an interpretation, or if they are unsure, elicit the evidence by asking, for instance, about the occasions on which a particular task has been performed. Interpretations without evidence are hunches and as such are more to do with the views and prejudices of the interviewer than they are to do with anything the candidate has said.

Endings

Candidates should always have the chance to ask questions, add anything they have forgotten and make any comments about the job or the interview. This ensures that the candidate feels that they have been treated fairly and has given the interviewers as much information as they can to allow a judgement to be made about their suitability for a job.

Unstated prejudices

A number of assumptions are often made about candidates without them even knowing they are being made. So, for example, the question of a woman's child care arrangements might not have been raised at an interview. However later when the candidates are discussed, assumptions might nevertheless be made about that woman's ability to work long hours or evenings, or what she would do if the child was sick.

Bias about appearance

Interviewers often make their judgement about the suitability of a candidate in the first two to four minutes of the interview. A major factor is appearance.

A `smart' appearance is often stated as a requirement for a job. It may very well be one, but opinions of what constitutes a smart appearance are likely to vary. For many years banks in this country would not allow their women staff to wear trousers to work. Similarly a man with dreadlocks may be thought not to be smart, even if he attends the interview in a suit.

Bias through gut feelings

Recruiters who speak of their gut feelings about candidates are rarely referring to any realistic objective assessment of candidates. They are more likely to be referring to their own emotions telling them that they like someone, or dislike them, or that a particular candidate is like, or very different from them. Few of these gut feelings have much to do with a candidate's ability to do the job.

Hidden agendas

The most common form of hidden agenda on interview panels is where the most powerful person on the panel has decided in advance who the successful candidate is going to be and the recruitment process is a sham. That is the most extreme. However there are many less well-defined hidden agendas. For example, if there is a very 'macho' culture in the department where the recruited person is going to have to work, the ability of the candidate to cope with this will often be tested in the interview and will effectively become an unwritten category on the person specification. This is not a requirement of the job; it is a requirement of those who currently do the job and those who manage them.

Horns or halo effect

If there is one answer or one aspect of a candidate a recruiter particularly likes or dislikes, they may not be objective about the other aspects of the candidate's performance, tending in the case of the halo effect to ignore or understate weaknesses, and the opposite with the horns effect. Each aspect of the person specification should be evaluated separately for this to be avoided.

Avoiding bias and prejudice

There are two clear ways of avoiding these kinds of bias and prejudice. First, the actual relevant and justified requirements of the job must be stated as explicitly and precisely as possible on the person specification. Wherever possible requirements that are simply matters of opinion should be avoided or defined in a way that is easily judged.

Secondly, where bias or prejudice is expressed by a member of the interview panel, either during the interview or in making a decision about a candidate, it is the responsibility of the others to challenge that prejudice and ensure that it can either be justified in terms of the job itself or directly from something the candidate has said. If it cannot, then it should be ignored.

People with disabilities

People with disabilities should not be asked at the interview whether their disability would prevent them from doing the job. They should have received sufficient information in advance, and have had the opportunity to discuss the job with someone within the organization, so that they can make up their own mind about their ability to do the job.

Their suitability for the post should be assessed regardless of their disability. If it is decided to offer them the job, they should then be asked whether their disability will mean that they need specific assistance, either in terms of special equipment, or personal assistance.

In the letter confirming the date and time of interview, candidates should also be asked to contact the organization if they have a disability and will need and equipment or assistance for the interview or for any of the other tests.

CHAPTER 10

OTHER METHODS OF ASSESSING CANDIDATES

Psychometric tests

Psychometric tests measure people's abilities and personalities. Since they are standardized, conducted according to set procedures, and objectively scored, they promise fair treatment for all. They may, in fact, be more fair and less subjective than other selection techniques such as unstructured interviews. Psychometric tests may however also cause indirect racial or sexual discrimination if they are badly designed or administered, improperly scored or not a suitable test of the qualities needed for the post to be filled.

In selecting candidates to fill a post, the most useful psychometric tests are those that fulfil the following three criteria: (1) they are specifically related to the post; (2) they measure the individual's ability to do the work; (3) they are reviewed regularly to be sure that the are both relevant and free from sexual and racial bias. As well as being unlikely to be the cause of indirect discrimination, tests that fulfil those three criteria will be more useful in selecting candidates.

As with all stages in the selection process, the first step is to refer back to the person specification to see what skills, knowledge, and abilities are required to do the job successfully. Then the tests that measure those abilities should be identified.

Choosing a test

When choosing a test, managers need to be sure that it is:
- professionally designed
- relevant to the vacant post
- both fair to the applicants and seen by them to be fair
- accompanied by a supporting manual
- not re-designed or modified.

A professionally designed test is less likely to be discriminatory because it has been scored by testing large numbers of people. These people are known as the norm group. They should be representative of the people that are to be tested by race, sex, and level of education. Generally, only a professional testing organization has the resources to test such large sample groups and the know-how to work out the scoring. Tests created in-house cannot hope to match them. But professionally designed tests are not totally problem free either. They too can be a cause of discrimination unless carefully chosen.

The manual that accompanies the test should provide the information that is needed to be sure that the test is both suitable for filling the job and for the applicant pool being tested.

When reading the manual, particular attention should be paid to the following points:
1) Statistics should be published to show that the test is both valid and reliable with results that are consistent time and again.

2)   The composition of the norm group should be close enough to the applicant pool so that the two can be compared. If it is not, the scoring will be invalid. Rather than trying to change the scoring, it is better to find a different test.
3)   The norm group should include women and a wide range of racial and ethnic groups to avoid problems of cultural or sexual bias.
4)   Information should be available on the fair use of the test in job selection. Men and women, for instance, might get different average scores on the test. The manual might offer suggestions about ways to overcome this difference.
5)   Evidence that in developing the test, the main ethnic and racial groups were included in test trials and validation studies.

Information should be requested where the manual does not deal with these issues. Where the answers are unsatisfactory, a different test might be more appropriate, or specialist advice from an occupational psychologist or other trained person may be sought.

Using the test

The best test in the world, however, will only be as fair as the person giving it. To measure accurately the applicants' abilities, aptitudes, knowledge or skills, the tests must be used correctly. They must be administered and scored according to the instructions. The staff supervising the test should receive training in test administration and scoring. Psychometric tests should never be administered by post.

Tests are not an infallible measure of applicants' abilities. It is therefore inadvisable to use absolute cut-off points unless there is a clear and proven relationship between performance on the test and in the job. Since they are only one selection measure among many, tests should be considered in relation to other sources of information about the candidate such as references, interviews, and job simulation exercises.

Test evaluation

After giving the tests and recruiting a candidate, the test itself should be evaluated to see if it was valid, both in terms of job selection and in terms of being non-discriminatory. Where large numbers of people are tested (more than 100), a formal validation study should be conducted. If the study reveals a sexual bias, a specialist may be able statistically to adjust the scores to eliminate the bias. A test that is revealed to contain bias on the grounds of race should not be used and the test's originators should be informed so that they can run further trials to eliminate the element of bias.

Most employers who use psychometric tests as part of their job selection procedure usually do not know what, if any, effect gender or race has on the scores. Because of this, they may run the risk of discriminating indirectly. If the test is shown to have had an adverse impact on some groups, the manager must prove that the test was justified.

To justify its use, the test must be shown to be:
- a fair reflection of the job;
- a measure of the skills or abilities required for that job;
- free of requirements for proficiency in irrelevant areas.

In addition, it must be shown that those who performed well on the test did just as well in the job. Without monitoring, a manager will not be able to justify the use of the test.

Explaining tests to candidates

Being sure that candidates are well-prepared for the test can to help avoid discrimination. All candidates should be sent a leaflet or brochure explaining the test procedure and including sample questions. Some employers offer candidates the chance to practice by taking a mock test. This can be especially helpful to applicants who are unfamiliar with testing procedures, either because they have been out of the workforce, did poorly at school, or come from a country where testing is not widely practised.

The time allowed to do the test can also be a factor in discrimination. Some people may need more time than others to complete the test. Assuming that the job does not involve performing the skill being tested under pressure of time, it may be possible to allow applicants more time. This might be fairer to all.

If well-conducted and appropriately used, tests can be less biased and more objective predictors of who will do the job well than many other selection methods. Choosing the right test in the first place is a vital part of fair recruitment and selection.

References

Many people feel that references from previous employers are worth very little. If the applicant was a valued employee in their previous job, the reference will reflect that. However, where they were not a good employee, the employer may be secretly anxious to rid themselves of them, so they will give them a good reference anyway. In addition, candidates themselves choose who to give as a referee and they are hardly likely to choose someone who is going to provide unflattering information. One further reservation is that referees express highly subjective opinions which, within the terms of a general reference request, they are not asked to support with evidence, and so what they say could be little more than personal prejudice.

There is however another school of thought: information about how an applicant actually did a previous job is infinitely more valuable than theoretical answers in an interview or in another form of assessment. Also, off-the-record information such as that often sought by headhunters, is likely to be more pertinent and accurate than guarded, formal statements.

Between these two extremes, references should be treated as a useful tool, principally for checking facts, within a broad and varied selection process.

Legal implications of references

References do have a legal status. Even if they are marked strictly confidential, they cannot in all circumstances be kept from the sight of the subject. Where a reference becomes an issue in any legal proceedings, for example, for discrimination or defamation, an industrial tribunal or court could order its disclosure. Where references are stored in computer records, they may become subject to disclosure under the Data Protection Act 1984.

It is possible, in theory at least, to bring an action against the referee for costs incurred where a candidate is appointed partly on the strength of a deliberately misleading reference made by the referee employer with the intention of getting rid of the candidate. Such actions are best avoided by a structured method of seeking references; resolution through litigation is unlikely to satisfy anyone. In any event, if a reference has been headed `without prejudice' or `without legal

108　Fair Recruitment and Selection

responsibility' the referee is explicitly denying responsibility for any decision taken on the strength of that reference.

If a candidate is offered a post and the offer is subsequently withdrawn on receipt of a bad reference, the employer may have to make a payment in lieu of notice. The way to avoid this is to offer all jobs `subject to satisfactory references'. A candidate should not start work until the reference has been received and checked both by personnel staff, and by the line manager of the person appointed.

The only statutory limitation on what may be said in references is about spent convictions under the Rehabilitation of Offenders Act 1974. This legislation was passed to protect ex-offenders from unfair discrimination. Employers should not take into account convictions for crimes which are `spent' when the person applies for the job. An employer should however ask candidates for information about any unspent convictions. The length of time it takes for the conviction to be spent varies and depends on the seriousness of the crime.

For some jobs, such as in social work and working with children, some convictions are never spent. It is good practice to ask the police to check for previous convictions for posts of this kind, and not to rely simply on disclosure by the candidate. Managers must avoid seeking information about spent convictions from referees.

Who should be referees?

There are obvious limitations on asking candidates to nominate their own referees. They will not nominate those who will paint an unflattering picture, even if that might be true. Prospective employers are therefore well-advised to seek references from all recent employers, certainly within the last five years, not just the one immediately preceding. They should also seek the views of the candidate's line manager. The personnel department may be able to provide standard factual information, but is unlikely to be able to give a detailed assessment of job competence.

A candidate's permission should be obtained prior to asking for a reference. Seeking references without consent would certainly be unethical. Reluctance on the part of a candidate to give consent is not necessarily an automatic disqualification from appointment. However the prospective employer will want to inquire about the reasons for the reluctance to give a particular previous manager as referee. A request for a blanket agreement to seek references from all previous managers is likely to bring to light any problems.

When should references be sought?

Prospective employers would ideally like references on all final shortlist candidates. In practice, however, candidates are understandably reluctant to give their consent to references being taken up before they know that they are going to be offered the job. This will alert their current employer to the fact that they are seeking employment elsewhere. Prospects in their current employment, should they fail to be appointed to the post they have applied for, may be jeopardized.

Information requested from referees

General requests for comments on a person's ability to do a job is unlikely to produce an illuminating reference. Prospective employers will want to seek two kinds of information: (1) checking of facts about previous employment; and (2) comments or judgements on ability and competence for the job sought.

It is good practice to ask the previous employers to confirm the information given by the candidate. For example: `Jack Hobbs has told us that he worked with you from January 1989 to December 1993 in the following posts.... His salaries were.... He gave the following reasons for leaving..... I would be grateful if you could confirm or correct this information.'

A prospective employer would also be well advised to ask for information about sickness record, time-keeping and any disciplinary matters.

In seeking information about competence and ability for the job sought, the prospective employer is not likely to get sufficiently specific information by simply sending a copy of the job description to the referees. This encourages referees to make comments on matters about which they may have no knowledge. It is better practice to ask the referee for specific information about the candidate's job performance in particular areas while in their employment, for example: `We would appreciate your comments on Jack Hobbs' ability to deal with the members of the public face-to-face and on the telephone, drafting reports, drafting correspondence, working with statistics etc...' Alternatively, `It would be particularly helpful if you could give us some examples or projects/tasks/achievements by the candidate in support of your judgements.'

Asking for information about a candidate's personality is not good practice. Most referees are unlikely to have the qualifications to make accurate assessments about personality. Secondly, personality is largely irrelevant for most jobs. The pertinent issues are behaviour and competence at work. Information about personality will always be subjective, and is quite likely to be based on prejudices or stereotypes and therefore not be accurate. The opinions may also reveal more about the referee than they do about the candidates.

Checking qualifications

A surprising number of people do not tell the truth about their qualifications in job applications. It is always good practice to ask for supporting evidence with application forms, even when the qualifications are not specifically required for the job being sought.

Verbal references

Seeking verbal references in person or on the telephone in an unstructured, informal, off-the-record manner is bad practice. It is simply a licence for prejudice. However, structured conversations and interviews, where the referee is asked a series of prepared, factual, specific questions in the areas highlighted above can be very useful. Many people find it easier to be open and informative verbally and the quality of the information gained may therefore improve.

If a referee has not answered specific requests for information in the reference, it is always advisable to ring and ask for their comments on the area not covered in the reference. Not commenting may simply have been an oversight. Alternatively, there may be some other relevant reason for a reluctance to commit an opinion to paper which would be useful to the future employer.

CHAPTER 11

SELECTING THE SUCCESSFUL CANDIDATE

Before considering or discussing whether a particular candidate meets the person specification or whether they should be offered the job, all interviewers should note the following key points:

1) Any quotes from the candidate that indicate their suitability or otherwise for the post, and why the interviewer has taken this inference from what they have said.
2) Interpretations that the interviewer has made from what the candidate has said and the evidence for that interpretation.
3) Anything else about the candidate which affects their suitability for the post, and why the interviewer has reached that conclusion.

Also see specimen interview record form in appendix A 5.

By making such a record interviewers can then compare notes and reach a consensus on the candidates' skills and abilities also taking into account the result of tests or references. Only once agreement has been achieved on this should the candidates be compared with the person specification and the job offered to the person who most exactly fits. Going straight to comparisons with the person specification leaves differences of opinion about candidates' suitability unresolved and therefore makes the process of reaching a decision less objective and potentially more controversial.

Scoring and grading systems need to be consistent and objective, otherwise they will be clumsy and ineffective. Marks out of ten will be judged differently by various interviewers. Adding up marks for different parts of the person specification as a way of making a decision can produce bizarre results, and abdicates the interviewers' responsibility to take a decision involving a judgement on all the facts. The grading system makes the decision, not the recruiters.

Assessing people for jobs should be a qualitative but objective process. This is different from turning it into a quantitative process, where those quantities themselves are open to subjective interpretation. The assessment system should be based on objectivity and consensus.

Often the weight of influence that one interviewer has over the outcome of a selection process is in direct proportion to the strength of their character. Thus the selection process is not an objective comparison of assessed competence, more a competition between the power of advocates. Different levels of authority and roles should be made explicit at the beginning so that all recruiters know how the final decision is to be made and on whose authority.

Interview panels are rarely democratic. Ideally everyone on the panel will agree. There may however be circumstances where they do not. Contingency plans should be laid for this at the beginning of the selection process: does anyone have the right of veto over individual candidates? Who has the final say?

Majority votes should be avoided. If an agreement cannot be reached, then the final decision should rest with the person who is going to manage the job, as they will be responsible for ensuring satisfactory performance. In reaching their decision, however, they should consider the views of all the recruiters, and be able to support the conclusion they have reached with evidence from the recruitment process.

There will be situations where there is more than one candidate who could be appointed to and successfully perform the job. It will, however, be rare for all the candidates who could be appointed to have exactly the same balance of strengths and weaknesses. In these circumstances recruiters should draw up a balance sheet of the strengths and weaknesses of the existing members of the team, and compare those with the strengths and weaknesses of the candidates who could be appointed.

The best candidate for the job will not be the one who most exactly replicates the existing workforce. It will be the one who best complements and supplements the skills, knowledge and experience of the existing workforce - the one who adds the greatest value to the organization. Adding value to the organization is, above all others, the most important objective in the recruitment and selection process and this will always be most effectively done by recruiting for diversity, not similarity, and that is the most powerful argument for fair recruitment and selection.

CHAPTER 12

MONITORING AND TARGET-SETTING

The best efforts to produce fairness in recruitment and selection must be monitored. The purpose of fair recruitment and selection is in the first instance to remove unfair bias. Secondly, it seeks to include groups or individuals who were previously under-represented in the workforce. Monitoring is designed to check whether that has worked. It is recommended by both the Commission for Racial Equality and the Equal Opportunities Commission. Organizations will want to monitor who is applying for jobs, who is being shortlisted, and who is successful.

Record-keeping and monitoring

All applicants for jobs should be asked to fill in a monitoring form. This should be separate from the application form, and anonymous. Many organizations have a monitoring form attached to the application form as a tear-off slip which is then separated by personnel staff before the application forms are passed on to the recruiters. An example of a monitoring form is given in appendix A 6. The form should collect data about membership of under-represented groups. Therefore the areas that are usually monitored are racial origin, gender and disability. In addition, some organizations also monitor disability and sexual orientation.

Some organizations now feel that ethnic origin information should be collected on the application form and be available to recruiters. Research indicates that recruiters having access to this information does not necessarily affect the outcome in terms of the ethnic origin of the successful candidate. However, there remains a residual concern amongst many applicants, particularly those from black and ethnic minority communities, that the information, if available to recruiters, will be used unfairly against them. It is, therefore, still probably advisable for the ethnic origin information to be collected separately so that assurances about confidentiality can be given to applicants.

Once these forms have been returned, all too often organizations simply collect this data and very little else happens to it. This is record-keeping not monitoring. Monitoring implies comparing the data collected with external benchmarks, for example, the breakdown of the population in the local catchment area. This population data is available for ethnic origin from the census. It is advisable for organizations to use the same categories as are on the census for ease of comparison.

If the numbers of people applying, being shortlisted or being selected do not reflect the local population, the reasons need to be sought, and some possibilities have been discussed earlier in this guide - the perception that the organization is a 'white' organization, or that the job is only suitable for men, or the lack of suitably qualified black or female candidates. The reasons for the lack of applications or shortlisted or successful candidates will define the corrective action that is necessary. Possibly the wording or placement of advertisements needs changing, or possibly the organization should offer positive action training opportunities.

The results of record-keeping should be monitored regularly, ideally after each appointment. The results should be discussed with the recruiters, and decisions about what steps need to be taken in future should then be made and recorded. Once a year, personnel staff should produce an overview of all the recruitment in the last twelve months. This should be discussed by the strategic planners in the organization - the senior management group, the management committee or the board of directors. This should inform approaches to recruitment in the forthcoming year to redress any existing imbalances.

Targets

In order to focus the monitoring efforts some organizations, such as the BBC and others, have set themselves equality targets. These are not quotas, which would be illegal, but an expression of what an appropriately balanced and mixed workforce would look like, either across the organization as a whole, or within particular departments or grades. This `volume' target is matched with a time target: an indication of how long it should take to achieve a balanced or representative workforce. Managers can then employ recruitment strategies to achieve these targets, such as those already mentioned: positive action in advertisements or training.

A further development in target-setting has been where organizations have monitored immediately after applications for the post have closed. The make-up of the applicants can then be compared against a population benchmark. If the benchmark does not compare with the actual applicants, managers can then decide whether to proceed with the recruitment or whether to return to the market through another advertisement to seek a more representative field before shortlisting, interviewing or selecting.

PART III

APPENDICES

A Human Resources Documentation

Appendix A 1
Person specifications

PERSON SPECIFICATION FORM

Job title ....

Department ....Date...........................

Manager ....

		Rank order
Skills/abilities		
Experience		
Knowledge		
Competencies		

122 Fair Recruitment and Selection

Specimen person specification for Personal Assistant to the Chief Executive

1 Skills/abilities

1.1 Secretarial skills

a) word processing at 60 words per minute, using WordPerfect 5.1;
b) RSA 2 typing;
c) accurate, grammatically correct audio typing.

1.2 Written communication skills

a) concise, accurate, grammatically correct drafting of correspondence and reports and taking minutes.

1.3 Verbal communication skills

a) courteous, fluent, calm, concise, telephone manner;
b) assertiveness, negotiating and influencing skills in achieving tasks involving other people;
c) dealing with rudeness politely and assertively, staying calm when experiencing difficult behaviour from senior people;
d) smart personal presentation for public occasions.

2 Organizational skills

a) managing diaries;
b) co-ordinating work of others;
c) progress chasing;
d) forward planning;
e) deciding between competing priorities;
f) working to deadlines;
g) working unsupervised;
h) organizing large meetings/conferences;
i) ability to attend evening meetings.

3 Experience

3.1 Minimum one year's senior secretarial experience

a)   organizing meetings involving large numbers of people;
b)   working with competing priorities;
c)   working without supervision.

4 Knowledge

a)   identifying and handling confidential information;
b)   business protocol.

Appendix A 2
Application form
Private and Confidential

Position applied for	How did you hear of it?	Ref. no

PERSONAL DETAILS

Surname	First names
Present address	Permanent address (if different)
Home phone number	Work phone number (to be used with discretion)

EMPLOYMENT RECORD
(starting with your own recent position)

Employer's name and address	Dates from/to	Job title and brief description of responsibilities (incl. salary details)
Current salary	Reasons for leaving/wishing to leave	

PROFESSIONAL QUALIFICATIONS/TRAINING

Place and method of study	Dates from/to	Courses/examinations taken and qualifications obtained	Grade

Please give details of any specialized formal or informal training you have received, not already covered

Please give details of any technical and other skills (eg, foreign languages, typing, use of office equipment) not already covered which could be useful to us

Membership of professional bodies and other organizations (relevant to the position applied for)   Date joined

SUPPORTING EVIDENCE

Using the job description provided, please use this section to outline where your knowledge, skills, experience and abilities are specifically relevant to the post. These may have been gained outside the workplace through activities and interests.

Tick box if you are continuing on a separate sheet ☐

How much notice is required by your present employer?

When would you be available to start work?

REFERENCES

Please give the names and addresses of referees from all employers from the preceding three years. If only one employer, or no previous employer, please also supply the name and address of a personal referee.

References will not be taken up without your permission

DECLARATION

I declare that, to the best of my knowledge, the information contained in this form is true and accurate. I understand that any misleading information could lead to termination of my contract if appointed.

Signed   Date

Appendix A 3

cv cover sheet

Private and confidential

Name
Position applied for

Using the job description provided, please use this section to outline where your knowledge, skills, experience and abilities are specifically relevant to the post. These may have been gained outside the workplace through activities and interests.

Tick box if you are continuing on a separate sheet ☐

DECLARATION

I declare that, to the best of my knowledge, the information contained in this form is true and accurate. I understand that any misleading information could lead to termination of my contract if appointed.

Signed   Date

Appendix A4

Applicants' short listing sheet

Vacancy: Vacancy No:

| Applicant's | | Selection criteria in ranked order | | | | | | | | | Short list decision |
No	Name										

Appendix A 5

Interview record form

Name of candidate ....

Vacancy..

Interview date.................Time.............1st/2nd interview

Interviewers..Room...................

Selection criteria (in ranked order)	Rating	Evidence
Comments:		

Rating:
3 fully meets criteria
2 substantially meets criteria
1 partially meets criteria

Recommendation:
SR strongly recommended
R recommended
P possible
NR not recommended

Action: Hold/Awaiting selection test results/Keep on file/Reject (give reason)

....

Make offer.......................................Start date.......................................

Appendix A 6
Equal opportunities monitoring form

This organization is committed to an equal opportunities policy to ensure that applicants are not discriminated against on the grounds of age, sex, ethnic origin, colour, disability or any other irrelevant criteria.

We would therefore be grateful if you would complete and return this section of the application form in the pre-paid envelope supplied to help us monitor the effectiveness of the policy.

This information will be treated in the strictest confidence and is not part of the selection process. Recruiters will not have access to this information

Position applied for..

Department..

1 Date of birth..............................

 Please answer by placing an x in the appropriate box.

2 Sex: ☐ Male ☐ Female

3 Ethnic origin:
 I would describe my ethnic origin as:
 ☐ Bangladeshi ☐ Chinese
 ☐ Black-African ☐ Indian
 ☐ Black-Caribbean ☐ Pakistani
 ☐ Black-Other ☐ White
 ☐ Other* (please specify)

* Other - persons originating from countries not included in the above categories, or persons whose parents are of differing origins, who do not choose to classify themselves elsewhere.

132 Fair Recruitment and Selection

4 Disability

Do you have a disability? ☐ Yes ☐ No

Are you registered disabled? ☐ Yes ☐ No

Full name..

Signature..................................... Date...............................

Appendix B

Codes of Practice

Appendix B1: Extracts on recruitment and selection from the Commission for Racial Equality's race relations code of practice on employment.

Advertisements

1.5 When advertising job vacancies it is unlawful for employers:
to publish an advertisement which indicates, or could reasonably be understood as indicating, an intention to discriminate against applicants from a particular racial group. (For exceptions see the section 29 of the Race Relations Act (RRA)).

1.6 It is therefore recommended that:
a) employers should not confine advertisements unjustifiably to those areas or publications which would exclude or disproportionately reduce the numbers of applicants of a particular racial group;
b) employers should avoid prescribing requirements such as length of residence or experience in the UK and where a particular qualification is required it should be made clear that a fully comparable qualification obtained overseas is as acceptable as a UK qualification.

1.7 In order to demonstrate their commitment to equality of opportunity it is recommended that where employers send literature to applicants, this should include a statement that they are equal opportunity employers.

Employment agencies

1.8 When recruiting through employment agencies, job centres, careers offices and schools, it is unlawful for employers:

a)   to give instructions to discriminate, for example by indicating that certain groups will or will not be preferred (for exceptions see section 30 RRA)

b)   to bring pressure on them to discriminate against members of a particular racial group (for exceptions see section 31 RRA)

1.9 In order to avoid indirect discrimination it is recommended that employers should not confine recruitment unjustifiably to those agencies, job centres, careers offices and schools which, because of their particular source of applicants, provide only or mainly applicants of a particular racial group.

Other sources

1.10 It is unlawful to use recruitment methods which exclude or disproportionately reduce the numbers of applicants of a particular racial group and which cannot be shown to be justifiable. It is therefore recommended that employers should not recruit through the following methods:

a)   recruitment, solely or in the first instance, through the recommendations of existing employees where the workforce concerned is wholly or predominantly white or black and the labour market is multiracial;

b)   procedures by which applicants are mainly or wholly supplied through trade unions where this means that only members of a particular racial group, or a disproportionately high number of them, come forward.

Sources for promotion and training

1.11 It is unlawful for employers to restrict access to opportunities for promotion or training in a way which is discriminatory (sections 4 and 8 RRA). It is therefore recommended that:

a) job and training vacancies and the application procedure should be made known to all eligible employees, and not in such a way as to exclude or disproportionately reduce the numbers of applicants from a particular racial group.

Selection processes

1.12 It is unlawful to discriminate, not only in recruitment, promotion, transfer and training, but also in the arrangements made for recruitment and in the ways of affording access to opportunities for promotion, transfer or training (sections 4 and 28 RRA).

Selection criteria and tests

1.13 In order to avoid direct or indirect discrimination it is recommended that selection criteria and tests are examined to ensure that they are related to job requirements and are not unlawfully discriminatory. For example:

a) a standard of English higher than that needed for the safe and effective performance of the job or clearly demonstrable career pattern should not be required, or a higher level of educational qualification than is needed;

b) in particular, employers should not disqualify applicants because they are unable to complete an application form unassisted unless personal completion of the form is a valid test of the standard of English required for safe and effective performance of the job;

c) overseas degrees, diplomas and other qualifications which are comparable with UK qualifications should be accepted as equivalent, and not simply be assumed to be of an inferior quality;

d) selection tests which contain irrelevant questions or exercises on matters which may be unfamiliar to racial minority applicants should not be used (for example, general knowledge questions on matters more likely to be familiar to indigenous applicants);

e) selection tests should be checked to ensure that they are related to the job's requirements, ie, an individual's test markings should measure ability to do or train for the job in question.

Treatment of applicants for shortlisting, interviewing and selection

1.14 In order to avoid direct or indirect discrimination it is recommended that:

a) Gate, reception and personnel staff should be instructed not to treat casual or formal applicants from particular racial groups less favourably than others. These instructions should be confirmed in writing.

b) In addition, staff responsible for shortlisting, interviewing and selecting candidates should be:
– clearly informed of selection criteria and of the need for their consistent application;
– given guidance or training on the effects which generalised assumptions and prejudices about race can have on selection decisions;

- made aware of the possible misunderstandings that can occur in interviews between persons of difference cultural background;
c) wherever possible, shortlisting and interviewing should not be done by one person alone but should at least be checked at a more senior level.

Genuine occupational qualification

1.15 Selection on racial grounds is allowed in certain jobs where being of a particular racial group is a genuine occupational qualification for that job. An example is where the holder of a particular job provides persons of a racial group with personal services promoting their welfare, and those services can most effectively be provided by a person of that group (section 5 and 5(2)(d) RRA).

Transfers and training

In order to avoid direct or indirect discrimination it is recommended that:
a) staff responsible for selecting employees for transfer to other jobs should be instructed to apply selection criteria without unlawful discrimination;
b) industry or company agreements and arrangements of custom and practice on job transfers should be examined and amended if they are found to contain requirements or conditions which appear to be indirectly discriminatory. For example, if employees of a particular racial group are concentrated in particular sections, the transfer arrangements should be examined to see if they are unjustifiably and unlawfully restrictive and amended if necessary;

c) staff responsible for selecting employees for training whether induction, promotion or skill training should be instructed not to discriminate on racial grounds;
d) selection criteria for training opportunities should be examined to ensure that they are not indirectly discriminatory.

Appendix B2: Extracts on recruitment and selection from the Equal Opportunities Commission's code of practice on employment

Recruitment

12 It is unlawful, unless the job is covered by an exception, to discriminate directly or indirectly on the grounds of sex or marriage:
– in the arrangements made for deciding who should be offered a job
– in any terms of employment
– by refusing or omitting to offer a person employment (section 6(1) of the Sex Discrimination Act (SDA)).

13 It is therefore recommended that:
a) each individual should be assessed according to his or her personal capability to carry out a given job. It should not be assumed that men only or women only will be able to perform certain kinds of work;
b) any qualifications or requirements applied to a job which effectively inhibit applications from one sex or from married people should be retained only if they are justifiable in terms of the job to be done (section 6(1) and section 1(1) or section 3(1) SDA);
c) any age limits should be retained only if they are necessary for the job. An unjustifiable age limit could constitute unlawful indirect discrimination, for example, against women who have taken time out of employment for child-rearing;

d) where trade unions uphold such qualifications or requirements as union policy, they should amend that policy in the light of any potentially unlawful effect.

Genuine occupational qualifications

14 It is unlawful, except for certain jobs when a person's sex is a genuine occupational qualification (GOQ) for that job, to select candidates on the grounds of sex (section 7 SDA).

15 There are very few instances in which a job will qualify for a GOQ on the ground of sex. However, exceptions may arise, for example, where considerations of privacy and decency or authenticity are involved. The SDA expressly states that the need of the job for strength and stamina does not justify restricting it to men. When a GOQ exists for a job, it applies also to promotion, transfer, or training for that job, but cannot be used to justify a dismissal.

16 In some instances, the GOQ will apply to some of the duties only. A GOQ will not be valid, however, where members of the appropriate sex are already employed in sufficient numbers to meet the employer's likely requirements without undue inconvenience. For example, in a job where sales assistants may be required to undertake changing room duties, it might not be lawful to claim a GOQ in respect of all the assistants on the grounds that any of them might be required to undertake changing room duties from time to time.

17 It is therefore recommended that:
- A job for which a GOQ was used in the past should be re-examined if the post falls vacant to see whether the

GOQ still applies. Circumstances may well have changed, rendering the GOQ inapplicable.

Sources of recruitment

18 It is unlawful, unless the job is covered by an exception:

– to discriminate on grounds of sex or marriage in the arrangements made for determining who should be offered employment whether recruiting by advertisements, through employment agencies, job centres, or career offices;

– to imply that applications from one sex or from married people will not be considered (section 6(1) SDA);

– to instruct or put pressure on others to omit to refer for employment people of one sex or married people unless the job is covered by an exception (sections 39 and 40 SDA);

It is also unlawful when advertising job vacancies

– to publish or cause to be published an advertisement which indicates or might reasonably be understood as indicating an intention to discriminate unlawfully on grounds of sex or marriage (s38 SDA).

19 It is therefore recommended that:

Advertising

a) job advertising should be carried out in such a way as to encourage applications from suitable candidates of both sexes. This can be achieved both by wording of the advertisements and, for example, by placing advertisements in publications likely to reach both sexes. All advertising material and accompanying literature relating to employment or training issues should be reviewed to ensure that it avoids presenting men and women in stereotyped roles. Such stereotyping tends to perpetuate sex segregation in jobs and can also lead people of the opposite sex to believe that they would be unsuccessful in applying for particular jobs;

b) where vacancies are filled by promotion or transfer, they should be published to all eligible employees in such a way that they do not restrict applications from either sex;

c) recruitment solely or primarily by word of mouth may unnecessarily restrict the choice of applicants available. The method should be avoided in a workforce predominantly of one sex, if in practice it prevents members of the opposite sex from applying;

d) where applicants are supplied through trade unions and members of one sex only come forward, this should be discussed with the unions and an alternative approach adopted.

Careers Service/schools

20 When notifying vacancies to the Careers Service, employers should specify that these are open to both boys and girls. This is especially important when a job has traditionally been done exclusively or mainly by one sex. If dealing with single sex schools, they should ensure, where possible, that both boys' and girls' schools are approached; it is also a good idea to remind mixed schools that jobs are open to boys and girls.

Tests

21 (a) If selection tests are used, they should be specifically related to job and\or career requirements

142 Fair Recruitment and Selection

and should measure an individual's actual or inherent ability to do or train for the work or career.

(b) Tests should be reviewed regularly to ensure that they remain relevant and free from any unjustifiable bias, either in content or in scoring mechanism.

Applications and interviewing

22 It is unlawful, unless the job is covered by an exception, to discriminate on grounds of sex or marriage by refusing or deliberately omitting to offer employment (section 6 SDA).

23 It is therefore recommended that:

a) employers should ensure that personnel staff, line managers and all other employees who may come into contact with job applicants, should be trained in the provisions of the SDA, including the fact that it is unlawful to instruct or put pressure on others to discriminate;

b) applications from men and women should be processed in exactly the same way. For example, there should not be separate lists of male and female or married and single applicants. All those handling applications and conducting interviews should be trained in the avoidance of unlawful discrimination and records of interviews kept, where practicable, showing why applicants were or were not appointed;

c) questions should relate to the requirements of the job. Where it is necessary to assess whether personal circumstances will affect performance of the job (for example, where it involves unsocial hours or extensive travel) this should be discussed objectively without detailed questions based on

Appendix B2 143

assumptions about marital status, children and domestic obligations. Questions about marriage plans or family intentions should not be asked, as they could be construed as showing bias against women. Information necessary for personnel records can be collected after a job offer has been made.

APPENDIX C
GLOSSARY

Definitions of the key concepts used in this guide are set out below.

Prejudice
Attitudes, opinions or feelings formed beforehand without informed knowledge. These are likely to be sustained even in the face of evidence to the contrary.

Stereotypes
Making judgements or statements about qualities of individuals which are then generally attributed to everyone in the groups of which they are a member.

Discrimination
Treating people differently and unfairly because of the group they belong to, without regard to the qualities or identity of the individual.

Indirect discrimination
Applying a condition or requirement to the provision of jobs, services, or goods, which adversely affects a particular racial group, sex, or other group, and cannot be justified on any other legitimate grounds. The discrimination may occur whether or not there was an intention to discriminate.

Passive discrimination
Passive discrimination occurs when unfair disadvantage befalls individuals or groups as a result of what organizations omit to do, rather than what they actively or deliberately do.

Black people

Black used until the 1960s to be a term of abuse. At that time it was appropriated by black people and turned into a term of pride. This is summed up by phrases from the time like 'black is beautiful.' Most African and Caribbean people and people from the Indian sub-continent now prefer it to the term coloured.

People with disabilities

A disability is one aspect of a person's identity. It is not the only important thing about that individual. It is therefore misleading to refer to disabled people. People with disabilities is a more accurate description. Disability need not be visible, or related to mobility. Disabilities may result in an inability to do certain actions or functions. Having a disability may also imply the ability to do some tasks with assistance.

INDEX

AIDS
    case study, 31–32
Advertising. *See* Job advertising
Agencies
    candidates, sources of, 62–63
    code of practice, 134
Appearance
    bias about, 99
Application
    advertisement which deters,
        68–69
    code of practice, 142–143
    forms, 65, 90, 124–127
Assessment centre
    evaluating, 86–87
    planning, 80–81
    running, 80–81
Avoiding bias and prejudice, 101

Behaviour
    interview, preparing for, 91
Bias
    appearance, about, 99
    avoiding, 101
    gut feelings, through, 100
    interview questions, in, 97–98

Black people
    meaning, 145

Candidates
    application forms, 65
    attracting field of, 57–66
    curricula vitae, 66
    discriminatory practice, 59
    information to inquirers, 64
    internal versus external
        advertising, 58–59
    references. *See* References
    sources of,
        agencies, 62–63
        colleges, 59
        consultants, 62–63
        job centre, 61
        journals, 63–64
        newspapers, 63–64
        positive action training
            scheme, 60–61
        schools, 59
        training scheme, 59–61
        university appointment
            board, 61–62

Index 147

Candidates—*contd*
  successful, selection of, 112–114
  tests. *See* Tests
  word of mouth, recruitment by, 59
Career development
  link between fair recruitment and, 12–13
Careers service
  code of practice, 141
Case studies, 30–35
Checking qualifications, 111
Civil service
  case study, 31
Closed questions at interview, 95
Codes of practice, 133–143
Colleges
  candidates, sources of, 59
Commission for Racial Equality (CRE)
  Race Relations Act 1976, enforcement of, 16–17
Community networks
  advertising through, 74
Company
  disabled person, responsibility towards, 22
Competencies
  training for recruiters, required for, 40–41
Consultants
  candidates, sources of, 62–63
Contents summary, 2–3
Creating rapport, 91
Curricula vitae
  cover sheet, 128
  preparation of, 66

Decision-making process
  interview, preparing for, 90
Designated employment scheme
  meaning, 21

Disabled person
  advertising for, 74
  companies, responsibilities of, 22
  designated employment scheme, 21
  Disabled Persons (Employment) Act 1944, 20–22
  discrimination against, 20–21
  employers, responsibilities of, 21
  interviewing, 101
  job description, 21
  meaning, 145
Discrimination
  candidates, attracting field of, 59
  disabled person, against, 20–21
  indirect, 144
  meaning, 144
  passive, 144

Employer
  disabled person, responsibilities towards, 21
  northern Ireland, in, duties placed on, 20
Employment
  agencies, 62–63 134
  designated scheme, 21
Ending of interview, 99
Enforcement
  Race Relations Act 1976, 16–17
  Sex Discrimination Act 1975, 18
Environment
  interview, preparing for, 90–91
Equal opportunities
  career development, 12–13

148 Index

Equal opportunities—*contd*
  commitment to, 7
  ethical considerations, 9–10
  interview questions, 96–97
  legal imperatives, 7–8
  monitoring form, 131–132
  positive action, 11
  positive discrimination, 11–12
  pragmatic reasons, 8–9
  training for recruiters, 36–37
Equal opportunities Commission
  (EOC)
  Sex Discrimination Act 1975,
    enforcement of, 18
Ethical considerations, 9–10
Evaluation
  assessment centre, of, 86–87
  tests, of, 105
External advertising, 58–59

First question at interview, 93–
  94
Follow-up questions at
  interview, 94–95
Forms
  application, 65, 90, 124–127
  equal opportunities
    monitoring, 131–132
  interview record form, 130
  person specification, 121

Genuine occupational
  qualifications
  advertising and, 25–27
  case studies, 33–35
  code of practice, 137, 139–140
  meaning, 24–25
  recruitment and selection,
    impact on, 25
Glossary, 144–145
Gut feelings
  bias through, 100

HIV
  case study, 31–32
Harassment
  racial, 19
  sexual, 19
Health authority
  case study, 33
Hidden agendas, 100
Horns or halo effect, 100
How-to questions at interview,
  96

Indirect discrimination
  meaning, 144
Information
  inquirers, to, 64
  referees, requested from, 109–
    111
Internal advertising, 58–59
Interviewing
  appearance, bias about, 99
  avoiding bias and prejudice,
    101
  bias,
    appearance, about, 99
    avoiding, 101
    gut feelings, through, 100
    questions, in, 97–98
  code of practice, 136–137,
    142–143
  disabled person, 101
  discrimination and, 27
  endings, 99
  generally, 88
  gut feelings, bias through, 100
  hidden agendas, 100
  horns or halo effect, 100
  interview panel members, 88–
    89
  listening skills, 98
  prejudice,
    avoiding, 101
    unstated, 99

Index 149

Interviewing—*contd*
  preparing for interview,
    application forms, 90
    behaviour, 91
    creating rapport, 91
    decision-making process, 90
    environment, 90–91
    openings, 92
    person specification, 89–90
  questions,
    bias in, 97–98
    closed, 95
    equal opportunities, 96–97
    first, 93–94
    follow-up, 94–95
    generally, 93
    how-to, 96
    leading, 95–96
    open, 94
  record form, 130
  unstated prejudices, 99

Job advertising
  advertisement which deters
    application, 68–69
  code of practice, 133, 140–141
  community networks,
    through, 74
  disabled person, 74
  external, 58–59
  genuine occupational
    qualifications and, 25–27
  information, 67–68
  internal, 58–59
  members of particular race or
    sex, 73–74
  purposes, 67
  targeted, 69–73
Job analysis
  areas to be analysed, 46–50
  continuous improvement, 46
  importance of, 45
  skipping, 45–46

Job centres
  candidates, sources of, 61
Job description
  disabled person who meets, 21
  drafting, 53–54
  generally, 53
  person specification, 54–56
Journals
  candidates, sources of, 63–64

Law and practice
  application of law, 15
  case studies, 30–35
  Disabled Persons
    (Employment) Act 1944,
    20–22
  equal opportunities policies, 7–
    8
  Fair Employment (Northern
    Ireland) Act 1989, 19–20
  generally, 14–15
  genuine occupational
    qualifications, 24–27
  illegal discrimination, 15
  interviews, 27
  positive action, 29–30
  Race Relations Act 1976,
    enforcement, 16–17
    races covered by, 16
    shared provisions with Sex
      Discrimination Act 1975,
      18–19
  racial discrimination, meaning,
    15–16
  references, legal implications
    of, 107–108
  selection, 27–29
  Sex Discrimination Act 1975,
    enforcement, 18
    permissible discrimination,
      17–18
    sex discrimination, meaning,
      17

150　Index

Law and practice—*contd*
  Sex Discrimination Act 1975—
    contd
    shared provisions with Race
      Relations Act 1976, 18–
      19
    wages, 17
    unlawful discrimination in
      recruitment, 22–24
Leading questions at interview,
  95–96
Length of shortlist, 76
Listening skills, 98

Monitoring
  equal opportunities
    monitoring form, 131–132
  generally, 115
  record-keeping, 115–117
  target-setting, 117–118

Newspapers
  candidates, sources of, 63–64
Northern Ireland
  employers, duties placed on,
    20
  Fair Employment (Northern
    Ireland) Act 1989, 19–20

Open questions at interview, 94
Opening interview, 92

Passive discrimination
  meaning, 144
Person specification
  checklist, 54–56
  drafting, 54–56
  form, 121
  interview, preparing for, 89–
    90
  specimen, 122–123

Person with disability. *See*
  Disabled person
Planning assessment centre, 80–
  81
Positive action
  equal opportunities, on, 11
  training scheme, 60–61
  under-representation and, 29–
    30
Positive discrimination, 11–12
Pragmatic reasons for equal
  opportunities policies, 8–9
Prejudice
  avoiding, 101
  meaning, 144
  unstated, 99
Preparing for interview. *See*
  Interviewing
Promotion
  code of practice, 135
Psychometric tests
  choosing, 103–105
  evaluation, 105
  explaining to candidates, 106
  generally, 102–103

Qualifications
  checking, 111
Questions. *See* Interviewing

Race
  particular, advertising for
    members of, 73–74
Racial discrimination
  harassment, 19
  nature of, 15–16
  Race Relations Act 1976,
    enforcement, 16–17
    races covered by, 16
    shared provisions with Sex
      Discrimination Act 1975,
      18–19

Index 151

Racial discrimination—*contd*
  specific organizations, special
    duties placed on, 16
Record-keeping, 115–117
Recruitment
  agencies, 62–63
  code of practice, 138–139, 140
  colleges, 59
  consultants, 62–63
  discriminatory practice, 59
  job centres, 61
  journals, 63–64
  newspapers, 63–64
  positive action training
    scheme, 60–61
  schools, 59
  stereotyping in, 50–52
  training . *See* Training for
    recruiters
  training for recruiters, 37–38
  training schemes, 59–61
  university appointment
    boards, 61–62
  unlawful discrimination in,
    22–24
  word of mouth, by, 59
References
  checking qualifications, 111
  generally, 106–107
  legal implications of, 107–108
  referees,
    information requested from,
      109–111
    who should be, 108–109
  value of, 106–107
  verbal, 111
  when sought, 109
Running assessment centre, 80–
  81

Schools
  candidates, sources of, 59
  code of practice, 141

Selection
  code of practice, 135–137
  discrimination and, 27–29
  successful candidate, of, 112–
    114
  training for recruiters, 37–38
Sex
  particular, advertising for
    members of, 73–74
Sex discrimination
  harassment, 19
  nature of, 17
  permissible, 17–18
  Sex Discrimination Act 1975,
    enforcement, 18
    shared provisions with Race
      Relations Act 1976, 18–
      19
  wages and, 17
Shortlisting
  applicants' short listing sheet,
    129
  assessment centres, 80–81,
    86–87
  choosing right tests, 81–84
  code of practice, 136–137
  length of shortlist, 76
  techniques, 76–80
  weighting tests, 84–86
  who should shortlist, 75
Stereotypes
  meaning, 144
  recruitment, in, 50–52

Targets
  advertising, 69–73
  setting, 117–118
Tests
  choosing, 81–84, 103–105
  code of practice, 141–142
  evaluation, 105
  explaining to candidates, 106
    choosing, 103–105

152 Index

Tests—*contd*
  psychometric,
    evaluation, 105
    explaining to candidates,
      106
    generally, 102–103
  weighting, 84–86
Training
  code of practice, 135, 137–138
  recruiters, for. *See* Training for
    recruiters
  scheme. *See* Training scheme
Training for recruiters
  competencies required, 40–41
  equal opportunities, 36–37
  fair recruitment and selection,
    37–38
  generally, 36
  objectives of course, 39–40
  specimen programme, 38–39
Training scheme
  candidates, sources of, 59–61
  positive action, 60–61

Under-representation
  positive action and, 29–30
University appointment boards
  candidates, sources of, 61–62
Unlawful discrimination
  recruitment, in, 22–24
Unstated prejudices, 99
Users of guide, 2

Verbal references, 111

Wages
  sex discrimination and, 17
Women
  advertising for members of
    particular sex, 73–74
  case study, 35
Word of mouth
  recruitment by, 59